The Process

By

Gary C. Price

Thank You

Dear Reader,

Thank you for purchasing The Process!

Please share your feedback on social media using our hashtags and handle: #theprocess.

For additional resources, or to book the author to speak at your event, please visit: rempublish.com

Regards,
Remnant Media Publications

Remnant Media
PUBLICATIONS

The Process

Omega Church and Ministries Center

P.O. Box 960146

Riverdale, GA 30296

https://rempublish.com/

www.omegaministries.org

ISBN: 979-8-9892937-9-7

Published in the United States by Remnant Media Services & Publications

All rights reserved. No part of this book may be reproduced or transmitted in any form or by any means without permission from the author.

Table of Contents

Acknowledgement

I would like to thank all the individuals involved in the writing process who contributed to the development of ideas, concepts, revelations, and graphics contained in *The Process*. This book has sincerely been a labor of love designed to show people in the Body of Christ how God's plan to advance His people has been strategically designed to make sure we reach our optimum potential.

I want to thank Omega Church and Ministries Center, Inc. for the prayer support and sacrifices made by all those that helped publish this book. I'd also like to thank Tanicia Prioleau and the Remnant Media Services staff for their dedication and focus while providing media production, editing, and publishing services. Your proficiency and hard work will never be forgotten.

Lastly, I'd like to thank my wife, Barbara, for her prayer support and faithfulness in standing with me in ministry for over 36 years. A faithful companion and partner are more valuable than words can express. Thank God for a saved, sanctified, and Holy Ghost filled wife!

ABOUT THE AUTHOR

Gary C. Price

Pastor Gary C. Price is the Senior Pastor of Omega Church and Ministries Center in Atlanta, Georgia. He Ministers to the Body of Christ under an anointing that deals specifically with the bondage of the inner man.

Pastor Price believes the present-day church has lost the vision that Jesus Christ imparted to the Apostles before He departed to be enthroned with His Father. He also received the revelations of a prophetic voice calling the Church back to patriarchal authority and obedience to the Holy Spirit when listening to his words.

His ministry began in 1984 after God prophetically called him to remove barriers that Satan had constructed to separate God from His people.
The main obstacle to remove, he believes, is religious bondage to man-centered organizations. Therefore, he has diligently sought the Lord for guidance on how to go about initiating the end-time deliverances to set the Body of Christ free.

FOREWORD

Some books contain great information, others great inspiration. This book is wholly different - in these pages, you'll find simple yet profound revelation. Revelation that when applied can effectively alter the reader's course in life.

Once you discover the revelation of The Process, it brings light to what phase of the process you're in, if in fact you're in it.

There's not many qualified to expound on this topic like Gary C. Price. His labor of love over the last two decades as a Husband, Father and Minister of the Gospel has given him a depth of experience and knowledge.

Don't wait a second longer to discover the revelation of The Process.

-Rashid Tillis

INTRODUCTION
An Overview of the Process

The Process is a book that provides the insight necessary to understand not only what happens to Christians after salvation, but also reveals to us why these occurrences take place. To understand the truths contained in this book, readers must receive the revelations contained in two very important foundational scriptures which serve as the basis for every word contained herein. These two scriptures must be examined carefully in order to see the necessity for change after we receive Jesus Christ as our personal Savior. The first scripture is Romans 12:1-2 and reads as follows:

I beseech you therefore, brethren, by the mercies of God, that you present your bodies a living sacrifice, holy, acceptable to God, which is your reasonable service. And do not be conformed to this world, but be transformed by the renewing of your mind, that you may prove what is that good and acceptable and perfect will of God.

The second scripture is found in Ephesians 4:17-24:

This I say, therefore, and testify in the Lord, that you should no longer walk as the rest of the Gentiles walk, in the futility of their mind, having their understanding darkened, being alienated from the life of God, because of the ignorance that is in them, because of the blindness of their heart; who, being past feeling, have given themselves over to lewdness, to work all uncleanness with greediness. But you have not so learned Christ, if indeed you have heard Him and have been taught by Him, as the truth is in Jesus: that you put off, concerning your former conduct, the old man which grows corrupt according to the deceitful lusts, and be renewed in the spirit of your mind, and that you put on the new man which was created according to God, in true righteousness and holiness.

These two scriptures together reveal to us that God's plan after salvation centrally focuses on renovating us to allow the Lord to take up residence in our lives. This process of renovation is referred to as "transformation" in Romans 12:2. The word translated as transformation in this scripture is the Greek word *metamorphoo* which means to change form. The Bible informs us that the change that God seeks for us is generated by the changing of our minds. This change causes us to think differently resulting in Christians having a different perspective about our surroundings. Once a Christian accepts Jesus Christ as the Savior, the Holy Spirit begins the process of transformation to deliver us from this present evil age by elevating our thinking processes. This process is necessary for every person who comes to the Lord if we intend to reach our maximum potential in God's kingdom. The Bible tells us that a mind that has not undergone the transformation process will not be able to walk with the Lord nor obey His instructions. The following discourse found in Romans 8:5-8 reveals the problem to us:

For those who live according to the flesh set their minds on the things of the flesh, but those who live according to the Spirit, the things of the Spirit. For to be carnally minded is death, but to be spiritually minded is life and peace. Because the carnal mind is enmity against God; for it is not subject to the law of God, nor indeed can be. So then, those who are in the flesh cannot please God.

It is imperative that we understand the damage done to our minds while living in Satan's domain without the knowledge of God. As willing participants in Satan's insidious matrix, we were all brainwashed to believe that the world was our friend and that it had our best interest embedded in it. The devil designed the world systems to enslave us. We accepted daily inputs from the world which locked our minds into his systems of control. These evil influences became spiritual programs that led us to do and think things that human beings would never engage in apart from the inspirations of the Satanic kingdom. The Bible states that "to be carnally minded is death" and "the carnal mind is enmity against God; for it is not subject to the law of God, nor indeed can be"; therefore, it becomes evident that the carnal mind is the problem embedded within the Christian personality that must be overcome and defeated.

It is also important for us to understand exactly what the carnal mind has done to us and how it anchors us to this world. When the Bible speaks of the carnal mind, it is referring to a mind that is plugged into the world using the five carnal senses as tools to onboard information continuously transmitted from the terrestrial (earthly) environment. A mind bathed in sensual inputs is programmed to believe that the temporal world is the environment that sustains life, provides security, transmits emotional stability, and comforts the soul. The revelation of God, which comes through His Son, the Lord Jesus Christ, shows us that the world and the things contained in it are *not* the source of happiness or peace, but in fact, these worldly inputs give us a false sense of security that will eventually leave us hopeless. This is why the Bible provides us the following instructions found in 1 John 2:15-17:

Do not love the world or the things in the world. If anyone loves the world, the love of the Father is not in him. For all that is in the world—the lust of the flesh, the lust of the eyes, and the pride of life—is not of the Father but is of the world. And the world is passing away, and the lust of it; but he who does the will of God abides forever.

Yes friends, this world is not designed to be permanent, neither is it designed to accommodate Christians who are seeking eternal life. The scriptures tell us that the three chains that bind us to the world are the desires of the flesh, the desires of the eyes, and the pride associated with the life we live here. The word of God has the power to deliver us from this present evil world by transforming our minds to disconnect the soul from the inputs that have enslaved us all our lives. As previously mentioned in Ephesians 4, humans have been systematically chained to Satan's world systems because minds have not undergone the renewal process. The scriptures state emphatically that this renewal process takes place in the spirit of our minds; therefore, it is imperative to understand exactly what the spirit of the mind is.

The word spirit in the Bible is the Greek word *pneuma* which means to breathe or blow and has a basic meaning of air in motion, or breath as something necessary to life. In Greek tragedy, it is used of the breath of life, and it is the spirit described in the New Testament (Oxford University Press, 2023). The spirit of the mind is the esoteric part of humans that inspires our thoughts, actions, feelings, desires, and perceptions of reality. The spiritual environment that envelopes the mind determines the direction our lives take based on the programming that drives us. In order to walk with the Lord Jesus Christ daily, this area must be renewed by removing the spiritual debris that negates the mind of Christ from interacting with our minds. This is why the scriptures state in Romans 8 that "the carnal mind is not subject to the law of God, neither indeed can be". Basically, the mind must be radically renovated to obey the inspirations of the Holy Spirit as the domination of our five carnal senses decreases and is replaced by the promptings of the Holy Spirit within our human spirit. In chapter 1 we will begin to illustrate how this process takes place as we examine the process of

The Process

metamorphosis that changes a caterpillar into a butterfly. The process that changes an earthbound hairy little creature into a beautiful airborne entity best describes the inner changes that Christians undergo after being born again.

CHAPTER 1
The Butterfly

To begin our understanding of the process that all Christians must go through, we will first look at an excerpt from an article that explains the four stages that characterize the life cycle of a butterfly.

Excerpt from "How Does a Caterpillar Turn into a Butterfly?"

By Allan's Pet Center[1]

The Process

Stage 1: Egg

The butterfly's life starts in a small, round, or oval egg. The shape varies depending on the butterfly type. Most butterflies lay their many eggs on leaves. The eggs attach to the leaves with an adhesive fluid. A mother butterfly can lay hundreds of eggs at one time, as many will not make it to the final stage of metamorphosis.

---

[1] "How does a caterpillar turn into a butterfly?" n.d. (https://allanspetcenter.com/how-does-a- caterpillar-turn-

into-a-butterfly/)

The Process

Stage 2: Larva

Once the butterfly hatches from the egg, it becomes a larva. However, this larva stage is when the butterfly is in caterpillar form. The tiny caterpillar has small eyes, short legs, and antennae. It also has bundles of cells called imaginal discs that are waiting to turn into butterfly features, including long antennae and legs, as well as wings. However, the imaginal discs are prevented from growing by a constant source of juvenile hormones. These hormones will eventually trigger the third stage. The caterpillar spends most of this time eating, including the leaf it was born on. In fact, caterpillars can be quite picky when it comes to what leaf to eat. This is why the butterfly must lay the eggs on a leaf the caterpillar will eat. For example, monarch caterpillars only eat milkweed. Once the caterpillar eats, it grows – about 100 times more than when they first hatched. Some internal organs begin to change, though the imaginal discs continue to stay dormant. Monarch caterpillars reach full growth after about two weeks of eating. Since their exoskeletons don't stretch, they grow by molting or shedding their skin, several times, like a snake.

Stage 3: Pupa

During this third stage, the caterpillar is now ready for the next stage. Once the caterpillar is done eating and growing, there is a lack of juvenile hormones, which causes the caterpillar to form a silk cocoon or shiny chrysalis around itself and begin radically transforming into a gorgeous butterfly. The cocoon is often hidden under branches, in a bunch of leaves or even underground. This transformation is called complete metamorphosis, which we discussed above. From the outside, nothing appears to be happening, but the inside is completely different. The caterpillar dissolves into a soup-like substance using enzymes triggered by hormones. Its tissues, limbs, organs, and imaginal discs then begin changing. The discs move to their correct positions, and the caterpillar starts taking a new shape as a butterfly. It sprouts new colors, wings, long legs and antennae, better, larger eyes and other adult butterfly features. The mouth changes from a chewing mouth into a proboscis that sips nectar, as butterflies don't eat solid food. The metamorphosis takes place over a few weeks or months, and the caterpillar transforms into a completely new-looking insect.

Stage 4: Adult

The finished product and final stage end with a butterfly. The newly turned butterfly will break free from its cocoon. It will take some time to stretch its long legs and antennae and pump hemolymph (the blood-like substance of insects) into its wings so it can fly. The butterfly must also wait for the wings to dry and grow to their full size. Once that happens, the butterfly will fly off and find a new mate to start the process all over again. Some butterflies only live a few weeks while others can last for months.

As illustrated by the four stages of a butterfly's development, organic transformation is not an overnight phenomenon. After Christians are born again it takes time to change the thinking patterns that have dominated our lives over the years and caused us to operate in a paradigm that was diametrically opposed to God and His word. The carnal mind that has been programmed to receive inputs through the five carnal senses will tend to negate the instructions of God simply because the thinking processes are not synchronized to obey the instructions inspired by the Spirit of the Lord. This is why the Bible tells us in Romans 8, that "the carnal mind is not subject to the law of God, neither indeed can be." The scriptures reiterate this fact in Ephesians 2:1-3:

And you He made alive, who were dead in trespasses and sins, in which you once walked according to the course of this world, according to the prince of the power of the air, the spirit who now works in the sons of disobedience, among whom also we all once conducted ourselves in the lusts of our flesh, fulfilling the desires of the flesh and of the mind, and were by nature children of wrath, just as the others.

The statement "by nature children of wrath" is a very strong indication that the problem embedded within human souls is centrally focused on the presence of a rebellious nature that was inherited from Adam and Eve. This embedded nature is governed by what 1 Corinthians 2:13-16 calls "a natural man" which is in turn governed by a natural mind:

These things we also speak, not in words which man's wisdom teaches but which the Holy Spirit teaches, comparing spiritual things with spiritual. But the natural man does not receive the things of the Spirit of God, for they are foolishness to him; nor can he know them, because they are spiritually discerned. But he who is spiritual judges all things, yet he himself is rightly judged by no one. For 'who has known the mind of the Lord that he may instruct Him?' But we have the mind of Christ.

Again folks, we see this continual focus on the carnal mind as the culprit that is preventing us from receiving the maximum benefits from our salvation. The mind that has been programmed from years of sin will be inclined to continue thinking the way it has become accustomed to thinking – until it has been reprogrammed to think in alignment with God's word.

The Process

The word of God reveals the will of God to us; therefore, when the mind is alienated from the word of God it is impossible for it to carry out the will of God. The greatest enemy we must conquer is found within our own souls; namely, the rebellious, noncompliant, contrary carnal mind that has plagued humanity down through the centuries. A careful examination of the scriptures reveals that this embedded enemy of God has been the source of all the problems that have existed since Eve listened to the whispered words of Satan. These words inspired Eve to rebel against the government of God that was designed to protect her and keep her rightly aligned with the plans of God. Immediately after Eve rebelled against the Lord, she inspired Adam to join her in this satanically-inspired insurrection and the carnal mind was activated as God's enemy. Listen to the words of Satan in Genesis 3:1-6 as he tempted Eve to rebel against God's authority by promising her a better life if she joined his mutiny:

Now the serpent was more cunning than any beast of the field which the Lord God had made. And he said to the woman, "Has God indeed said, 'You shall not eat of every tree of the garden'?" And the woman said to the serpent, "We may eat the fruit of the trees of the garden; but of the fruit of the tree, which is in the middle of the garden, God has said, 'You shall not eat it, nor shall you touch it, lest you die.'" Then the serpent said to the woman, "You will not surely die. For God knows that in the day you eat of it your eyes will be opened, and you will be like God, knowing good and evil." So, when the woman saw that the tree was good for food, that it was pleasant to the eyes, and a tree desirable to make one wise, she took of its fruit and ate. She also gave it to her husband with her, and he ate it. Then the eyes of both were opened, and they knew that they were naked; and they sewed fig leaves together and made themselves coverings.

What was the first consequence of obeying the directives of Satan the rebel? Self-consciousness flooded their minds and souls. Yes friends, self-consciousness is the insidious curse that comes upon the carnal mind causing all the disastrous thinking, feelings, attitudes, fears, emotions, and misconceptions that define the life of a rebellious sinner. When Satan's nature influences the mind, it automatically begins to build defenses against the intrusion of God's word into the thinking processes, resulting in a tendency to be offended by Biblical truth. A person infected and affected by Satan's lies will automatically fight against anyone or anything that represents God as they opt to become agents that undermine the Kingdom of God. The curse of the carnal mind is evident throughout society today as we witness multitudes inspired by Satan's mind beginning to turn against God's word and His Son, the Lord Jesus Christ. The carnal mind, governed by the five carnal senses, is continually gathering inputs from the world and making decisions based on information transmitted by agents of Satan that usually have an evil intent. Inputs from Satan's world (which we refer to as the matrix), are designed to stimulate participation in terrestrial kingdoms organized by the devil as he pits himself against the Kingdom of God. These inputs lead to rebellion against God, and they also inspire what the Bible calls the works of the flesh as revealed in Galatians 5:19-21:

Now the works of the flesh are evident, which are:

adultery, fornication, uncleanness, lewdness, idolatry, sorcery, hatred, contentions, jealousies, outbursts of wrath, selfish ambitions, dissensions, heresies, envy, murders, drunkenness, revelries, and the like; of which I tell you beforehand, just as I also told you in time past, that those who practice such things will not inherit the kingdom of God.

Careful examination of these scriptures reveals that carnal minds have been programmed to engage in carnal activities that are diametrically opposed to God's laws and His Kingdom Principles; therefore, those who participate in these activities "will not inherit the kingdom of God." The works of the flesh are generated by satanically inspired thoughts that affect our desires causing rebellion against the Lord, as internal carnal inspirations detach us from righteous inputs provided by God's Holy Spirit. In this compromised state, obeying Satan becomes normal to Adam's lineage and living sinful lives of rebellion becomes normal to all those engaged in persistent anti-God revelry. Simply stated, the carnal mind ingests data from the world inspiring rebellion against God. Rebellion against God manifests as sinful acts against God's word and the Lordship of Jesus Christ. Unrestrained participation in sin causes the soul to wander further and further away from God until it becomes accustomed to living in sin and rebellion. In this state, the world becomes the domain that negates interaction with God and earth-bound existence is normal to those who have received carnal programming inspired by Satan, fallen angels, and demons. This programming shapes the life of an earth-bound caterpillar and it is the accepted way to live by humans held captive in Satan's terrestrial prison. We can only be liberated by being born again as God's incorruptible seed conceives a spiritual man within us equipped with a spiritual consciousness that desires to serve God. In chapter 2, we will examine how the incorruptible seed of the word regenerates us.

CHAPTER 2

Receiving The Incorruptible Seed

Since you have purified your souls in obeying the truth through the Spirit in sincere love of the brethren, love one another fervently with a pure heart, having been born again, not of corruptible seed but incorruptible, through the word of God which lives and abides forever, because "All flesh is as grass, and all the glory of man as the flower of the grass. The grass withers, and its flower falls away, but the word of the Lord endures forever." Now this is the word which by the gospel was preached to you. (1 Peter 1:22-25)

These verses of scripture found in 1 Peter tell us that after we are born again from incorruptible seed, the soul is purified by obeying the truth. The word of God has the power to bring our spirits back alive from the dead when we accept the Lord Jesus Christ as our personal Savior. God's word acts as spiritual semen that enters the human spirit reviving it from a life of sin and rebellion. When humans rebel against God, we are dead to God's heavenly kingdom and unable to relate to the commands and laws given to us through the word of God inspired by the Holy Spirit. Basically, humans out from under heavenly authority operate as Satanic agents that exist only to fulfill their sensual desires and seek pleasure at the expense of obedience to the Lord Jesus and His revealed will. Jesus Christ said that we are not able to serve Him if our spirits are dead in trespasses and sins because without the new birth, human beings are programmed by nature not to obey God. Jesus had a conversation with a man named Nicodemus that reveals this truth in John 3:

There was a man of the Pharisees named Nicodemus, a ruler of the Jews. This man came to Jesus by night and said to Him, "Rabbi, we know that You are a teacher come from God; for no one can do these signs that You do unless God is with him." Jesus answered and said to him, "Most assuredly, I say to you, unless one is born again, he cannot see the kingdom of God." Nicodemus said to Him, "How can a man be born when he is old? Can he enter a second time into his mother's womb and be born?" Jesus answered, "Most assuredly, I say to you, unless one is born of water and the Spirit, he cannot enter the kingdom of God. That which is born of the flesh is flesh, and that which is born of the Spirit is spirit. Do not marvel that I said to you, 'You must be born again.' The wind blows where it wishes, and you hear it, but cannot tell where it comes from and where it goes. So is everyone who is born of the Spirit." Nicodemus answered and said to Him, "How can these things be?" Jesus answered and said to him, "Are you the teacher of Israel, and do not know these things? Most assuredly, I say to you, we speak what we know and testify to what we have seen, and you do not receive our witness. If I have told you earthly things and you do not believe them, how will you believe if I tell you heavenly things? No one has ascended to heaven but He who came down from heaven, that is, the Son of Man who is in heaven. And as Moses lifted up the serpent in the wilderness, even so must the Son of Man be lifted up, that whoever believes in Him should not perish but have eternal life. For God so loved the world that He gave His only begotten Son, that whoever believes in Him should not perish but have everlasting life. For

The Process

God did not send His Son into the world to condemn the world, but that the world through Him might be saved." (John 3:1-17)

Nicodemus was a leader in the religious community when Jesus appeared on the scene, yet he had no understanding of the spiritual truths revealed through God's word. Twenty-first-century Christianity is suffering through the same problem simply because religion is the repository that accommodates the carnal mind and sensual inputs received from Satan's earthly kingdom. Sadly, most religious systems are designed to stimulate the sensual natures that have been programmed to receive the carnal impulses that make us the enemy of God. When the five carnal senses needed to live in the physical world become the primary tools used by the mind to process information, humans are ultimately flying blind because awareness of the spiritual aspects of life are no longer available to us. The state of the blinded mind is revealed to us in 2 Corinthians 4 by Apostle Paul as he writes:

But if our gospel is hidden, it is hidden to them that are lost: In whom the god of this world hath blinded the minds of them which believe not, lest the light of the glorious gospel of Christ, who is the image of God, should shine unto them. (2 Corinthians 4:3-4)

As revealed earlier in this book, the carnal mind is the enemy of God, and as such it is not able to receive inputs from the mind of God. This is the reason why the blinded mind stumbles through life antagonistically weaponized against the word of God and focused on self-preservation at the expense of eternal life. Carnal senses are designed to sustain carnal life by protecting it, informing it, guiding it, and detecting danger generated by the environment we live in. However, when these senses become the primary source of inputs apart from the Spirit of God, they become detrimental to our relationship with God. Human beings were designed to live from the inside out because our spirits were supposed to be inspired by God enabling us to be led by the Lord in complete obedience to heavenly instructions. When the soul gains superiority over the spirit, mankind instinctively will seek pleasure over obedience to the word of God resulting in internal chaos and confusion. The only way to correct this situation is to be born again by receiving the incorruptible seed of God's word which resurrects our spirit. This begins the process of transformation to reestablish a relationship with the kingdom of God. The process we speak of in the pages of this book is all about the growth and expansion of this regenerated life and the effect it has on our daily lives.

CHAPTER 3
Organic Transformation

I beseech you therefore, brethren, by the mercies of God, that you present your bodies a living sacrifice, holy, acceptable to God, which is your reasonable service, and do not be conformed to this world, but be transformed by the renewing of your mind, that you may prove what is that good and acceptable and perfect will of God. (Romans 12:1-2)

To understand the process of organic transformation, we must understand that God needs access to our human bodies to begin the transformation. Romans 12:1 instructs us to "present our bodies as living sacrifices" allowing the Lord to infiltrate the internal mechanisms that inspire us to think the thoughts that direct our lives. After we are born again, it is imperative that Christians immediately begin to understand the necessity of change. Many of us have been told repeatedly that God accepts us just like we are and that there are no special qualifications necessary to become a child of God. For years ministers have told people to "come just as you are" without any instructions given to individuals concerning what needs to happen once they get inside of the Kingdom of God. While it is true that we come to Jesus Christ as sinners totally dependent upon the grace of God found in the sacrificial offering of His Son on the cross, it is also just as important to be told what the Lord expects from us once we become members of His family. Christians rarely find ministers telling them that salvation is presenting your body back to God as a sacrifice after we've repented from sins committed using our bodies.

Jesus tells us in Mark 1:14-15 exactly what we have to do in order to be accepted into the Kingdom of God:

Now after John was put in prison, Jesus came to Galilee, preaching the gospel of the kingdom of God, and saying, "The time is fulfilled, and the kingdom of God is at hand. Repent, and believe in the gospel."

As the scripture reveals here, the requirement to enter the Kingdom of God is more than just believing because the Lord told us to "repent and believe the gospel."

Christians need to be instructed to repent and turn away from sins *before* attempting to believe the good news of Jesus Christ. In fact, without repentance, the ability to believe the gospel will be negated because the cares of this world will choke off the word and render it unfruitful as illustrated in Matthew 13:22:

Now he who received seed among the thorns is he who hears the word, and the cares of this world and the deceitfulness of riches choke the word, and he becomes unfruitful.

When the gospel is preached to unbelievers, they must be told that the world must be forsaken for sincere faith to be birthed in their hearts. If new converts are not told that this present evil world is the enemy of their faith, they will tend to try to live in two worlds simultaneously and end up hindering the organic growth of God's word embedded in their hearts. Christians who sincerely repent immediately find out that the Kingdom of God stands ready to receive them into God's family when the spiritual conditions have been met for the Lord's eternal word to be empowered in their life. For us to get a clearer understanding of what it means to repent, let's look at an article that explains repentance in detail.

You Must Repent Now and Believe the Gospel[1]

In the heart of the Christian faith lies a profound call to repentance. But what does it mean to repent? Is it simply remorse over past wrongdoings or is it something deeper? Let's delve into what repenting truly means and explore how it connects with the Gospel.

The Call to Repent Now

Throughout the Bible, we see a repeated invitation to repent now. The message is clear — the time for repentance is not in the future, but it is in the present moment. In Acts 3:19, we find an inspiring proclamation: "Repent, then, and turn to God, so that your sins may be wiped out, that times of refreshing may come from the Lord."

Repentance: The Biblical Perspective

When we attempt to define repent, it's important to understand its original biblical context. The term "repent" in the Bible is translated from the Greek word *metanoia*, which means "change of mind." Therefore, the meaning of "repent" encompasses not just feeling sorry for your sins, but a complete change in how one thinks and lives.

Repentance: More Than an Apology

Similarly, repentance also goes beyond mere regret over sins. In essence, repentance is a transformation of the heart and mind that leads to a change in behavior, guided by a profound understanding of God's will. This is seen in Luke 13:3: "I tell you, no! But unless you repent, you too will all perish."

What Is Repentance in the Christian Faith?

Answering the question, "What is repentance?", in the Christian context, we see it as a two-part process. First, recognizing and confessing your sins before God, and second, turning away from sinful behavior. Repentance signifies a shift from a self- centered life to a God-centered one.

The shift from a self-centered life is the most important

aspect of repentance because this change enables us to relate to the word of God in a whole new way. When human beings live a life centrally focused on self, we tend to focus solely on how to sustain our lives in the here and now at the expense of eternity. The self-centered life is a life totally governed by the five carnal senses and bathed in world consciousness. This kind of existence is totally separate from the Kingdom of God and easily influenced by Satan's inspirations and guidance; therefore, men and women chained to self-consciousness are not able to be subject to God's laws and principles.

---

[1] "You Must Repent Now," n.d. (https://info.gonow.org/you-must-repent-now-and-believe-the gospel/)

The Process

The selfish life is the life we inherited from Adam and Eve, and it is sustained by rebellion, pride, and stubbornness all under the influence and guidance of Satan's evil spirit. When people have not repented and turned away from sin, their minds are alienated from God and His word becomes strange and distant to them. Romans 8 gives insight concerning this condition as it speaks to us concerning the carnal mind:

There is therefore now no condemnation to those who are in Christ Jesus, who do not walk according to the flesh, but according to the Spirit. For the law of the Spirit of life in Christ Jesus has made me free from the law of sin and death. For what the law could not do in that it was weak through the flesh, God did by sending His own Son in the likeness of sinful flesh, on account of sin: He condemned sin in the flesh, that the righteous requirement of the law might be fulfilled in us who do not walk according to the flesh but according to the Spirit. For those who live according to the flesh set their minds on the things of the flesh, but those who live according to the Spirit, the things of the Spirit. For to be carnally minded is death, but to be spiritually minded is life and peace. Because the carnal mind is enmity against God; for it is not subject to the law of God, nor indeed can be. So then, those who are in the flesh cannot please God. (Romans 8:1-8)

Yes, indeed folks, the carnal mind is the enemy of God and if it governs our lives, we are not able to serve the Lord Jesus Christ in any capacity. In fact, everything we are writing concerning "the process" centrally focuses on the mind and the need for it to be completely metamorphosized to serve God and obey His commandments. As we read earlier in Romans 8, it is imperative that we have our minds transformed to affirm the good, acceptable, and perfect will of God. The word translated as "transformed" in this passage is the Greek word *metamorphoo* which means to change, transfigure, or transform. The passage instructs us that to fulfill the will of God, we must be renewed or renovated by having our minds transformed, which suggests a total upgrade in our thinking processes. Ephesians reinforces this concept in chapter 4, verses 17-24, which reveal to us the mystery surrounding what the Bible calls the "spirit of your mind".

The Process

This I say, therefore, and testify in the Lord, that you should no longer walk as the rest of the Gentiles walk, in the futility of their mind, having their understanding darkened, being alienated from the life of God, because of the ignorance that is in them, because of the blindness of their heart; who, being past feeling, have given themselves over to lewdness, to work all uncleanness with greediness. But you have not so learned Christ, if indeed you have heard Him and have been taught by Him, as the truth is in Jesus: that you put off, concerning your former conduct, the old man which grows corrupt according to the deceitful lusts, and be renewed in the spirit of your mind, and that you put on the new man which was created according to God, in true righteousness and holiness. (Ephesians 4:17-24)

To fully understand the mystery of transformation, we must evaluate Romans 12 along with Ephesians 4, because both passages deal with the mind as the central focus for change in a Christian's life. The scriptures reveal to us that the born-again experience is realized when an individual turns *away* from a life of sin in the world opting to turn *towards* a new life provided by a relationship with Jesus Christ. When we receive Christ as our Lord and Savior, the Holy Spirit regenerates our human spirit, and life from God is imparted to us, awakening the energy needed to become children of God. The revived spirit inside of us comes forth as an awakened entity that was in suspended animation unable to express itself while the body and soul were alive and thriving.

Essentially, our spirits are held as prisoners within the confines of our bodies because rebellious natures are at work within us inspiring sin and rebellion against the Lord and His word. When we are trapped in this life of sin, the carnal mind is the operating system that governs our activities as it maintains a consistent connection to Satan's kingdom, which is governed by fallen angels and demons. The book of Ephesians explains this connection well as it reveals the following:

And you He made alive, who were dead in trespasses and sins, in which you once walked according to the course of this world, according to the prince of the power of the air, the spirit who now works in the sons of disobedience, among whom also we all once conducted ourselves in the lusts of our flesh, fulfilling the desires of the flesh and of the mind, and were by nature children of wrath, just as the others. (Ephesians 2:1-3)

The phrase "by nature children of wrath" is very important here because it reveals the fact that our problems are found in a nature that is birthed in us because of rebellion. Sadly, most Christians are never taught that sinful activities are inspired by a sinful nature within their souls, so they never target the real cause of inner conflicts and torment. This inherited sinful nature is at the center of all of mankind's problems. Left unaddressed, this nature will slowly erode all the normal human functionalities of the soul. Romans 1 tells us that the end of this deterioration results in a mind that is totally depraved and unable to interact with God. Paul the Apostle outlines the steps into depravity as minds wander away from God's word:

For the wrath of God is revealed from heaven against all ungodliness and unrighteousness of men, who suppress the truth in unrighteousness, because what may be known of God is manifest in them, for God has shown it to them. For since the creation of the world His invisible attributes are clearly seen, being understood by the things that are made, even His eternal power and Godhead, so that they are without excuse, because, although they knew God, they did not glorify Him as God, nor were thankful, but became futile in their thoughts, and their foolish hearts were darkened. Professing to be wise, they became fools, and changed the glory of the incorruptible God into an image made like corruptible man—and birds and four- footed animals and creeping things. Therefore, God also gave them up to uncleanness, in the lusts of their hearts, to dishonor their bodies among themselves, who exchanged the truth of God for the lie, and worshiped and served the creature rather than the Creator, who is blessed forever. Amen.

For this reason, God gave them up to vile passions. For even their women exchanged the natural use for what is against nature. Likewise, also the men, leaving the natural use of the woman, burned in their lust for one another, men with men committing what is shameful, and receiving in themselves the penalty of their error which was due.

And even as they did not like to retain God in their knowledge, God gave them over to a debased mind, to do those things which are not fitting; being filled with all unrighteousness, sexual immorality, wickedness, covetousness, maliciousness; full of envy, murder, strife, deceit, evil-mindedness; they are whisperers, backbiters, haters of God, violent, proud, boasters, inventors of evil things, disobedient to parents, undiscerning, untrustworthy, unloving, unforgiving, unmerciful; who, knowing the righteous judgment of God, that those who practice such things are deserving of death, not only do the same but also approve of those who practice them. (Romans 1:18-32)

Pay special attention to the fact that this entire process culminates with the human mind entering a state called reprobation. Reprobation means condemnation to eternal punishment in hell and total rejection by God. A reprobate mind is the mind Satan received when he rebelled against the Kingdom of God long ago before Adam and Eve were called upon to repopulate the Earth. His mind is completely rotten to the core and unable to relate to the laws of God, the righteous standards of God, the truth of scriptures, or anything that relates to holiness, sobriety, decency, or honesty. When humans become reprobate, they are a living expression of Satan's insane depravity and his complete commitment to evil without any limitations. This is the nature that the Lord Jesus Christ saved us from, and it is this nature that inspires the minds and souls of those who continually rebel against God and His eternal word. This is also the nature that must be supernaturally transformed and renewed by interacting with the word of God, prayer, fasting, and continual praise and worship, along with a diligent separation from defiling elements that seek to undermine transformation.

Always remember, that organic transformation is necessary to live the Christian life and this transformation takes place in the mind. The process is designed to optimize the environment within the hearts of Christians allowing them to stay focused while undergoing this all-important transformational journey. This is a topic that is not addressed most times in Christian circles, but now it's time to deal with the embedded contagions within our souls by getting rid of hidden enemies embedded in the mind. Next, we will discuss what happens to us as transformation changes the way we think.

CHAPTER 4
Receivers and Transmitters

In this chapter, we will illustrate the characteristics of the mind by describing radio transmission and reception. Let's begin by defining a few terms.

Receiver: In radio communications, a radio receiver, also known as a receiver, a wireless, or simply a radio, is an electronic device that receives radio waves and converts the information carried by them to a usable form. It is used with an antenna.

Transmitter: A transmitter is a circuit that accepts signals or data input and translates them into a form that can be sent (transmitted), across a medium, usually over a distance. The medium can be wireless or wired.

Usually, mechanisms that can receive transmissions can also send them. For instance, your television, car radio, and cell phone can not only receive communication signals, but they can also transmit signals. To get a clearer understanding of how transmission and

The Process

reception work, let's look at radio waves and how they relate to communication between two different sources. Here we will reference an article written in Wikipedia that explains how radio waves and frequencies are used to communicate around the world:

Radio waves are a type of electromagnetic radiation with the longest wavelengths in the electromagnetic spectrum, typically with frequencies of 300 gigahertz (GHz) and below. At 300 GHz, the corresponding wavelength is 1mm, which is shorter than the diameter of a grain of rice. At 30 Hz the corresponding wavelength is
~10,000 kilometers (6,200 miles), which is longer than the radius of the Earth.

Naturally occurring radio waves are emitted by lightning and astronomical objects and are part of the blackbody radiation waves emitted by all warm objects. Radio waves are generated artificially by an electronic device called a transmitter, which is connected to an antenna that radiates the waves. They are received by another antenna connected to a radio receiver, which processes the received signal.

To prevent interference between different users, the artificial generation and use of radio waves are strictly regulated by law, coordinated by an international body called the International Telecommunication Union (ITU), which defines radio waves as "electromagnetic waves of frequencies arbitrarily lower than 3,000 GHz, propagated in space without an artificial guide". The radio spectrum is divided into several radio bands based on frequency, allocated to different uses.[1]

As stated in the Wikipedia article “the radio spectrum is divided into several radio bands based on frequency, allocated to different uses.” In physics, frequency is defined as the number of waves that pass a fixed point in a unit time. Simultaneous Transmit and Receive (a.k.a. STAR)

The Process

---

[1] "Radio Wave," n.d. (https://en.wikipedia.org/wiki/Radio_wave#:~:text=Radio%20waves%20are%20)

antennas can send and receive a signal at the same time on the same frequency and can double communication data rates in wireless point-to-point communications. Transmission and reception of radio waves allow individuals to communicate with each other from locations that are extremely distant from each other. If both parties are on the same frequency, the messages sent and received will be clearly understood and easily interpreted, but if the frequency is not the same, then messages will be unreceived or lost in transmission.

Human Transmitters and Receivers

If we understand the necessity of having the same frequency when communicating at great distances, then the necessity of renewing the mind becomes evident. Again, referring to Romans 12:1-2, the Bible instructs us to "be transformed by the renewing of our minds." The inner metamorphosis described in the Bible is the change necessary to make our minds receptive to the spiritual transmissions emanating from the throne of God.

Romans 8:6-8 informs us that to "be carnally minded is

death, but to be spiritually minded is life and peace. Because the carnal mind is enmity against God; for it is not subject to the law of God, nor indeed can be. So then, those who are in the flesh cannot please God." Based on these scriptures, we can conclude that the carnal mind operates on a different spiritual frequency than the spiritual mind making it unable to communicate with God and alienating the carnal mind from God's laws and commandments. This condition is reinforced in Ephesians 4:17-19, which states, "This I say, therefore, and testify in the Lord, that you should no longer walk as the rest of the Gentiles walk, in the futility of their mind, having their understanding darkened, being alienated from the life of God, because of the ignorance that is in them, because of the blindness of their heart; who, being past feeling, have given themselves over to lewdness, to work all uncleanness with greediness." Listen very carefully to those words, "being alienated from the life of God," which indicates the mind has been made to feel estranged, separated, or withdrawn from God and His word. Alienation occurs when a person withdraws or becomes isolated from their environment or from other people. People who show symptoms of alienation will often reject loved ones or society. They may also show feelings of distance and estrangement, including from their own emotions. An alienated mind becomes an enemy of God because it is inspired to stand against the Lord's dominion and authority while choosing to follow the dictates of the five carnal senses.

If we synthesize the revelations found in Romans 8 with the information provided in Ephesians 4, the mystery of mental alienation becomes obvious. The alienated, carnal mind is connected to the five carnal senses that are used by human souls to interact with the physical world. Basically, everything we see, hear, touch, taste, and smell enters the soul through these five carnal receptors that provide guidance and protection for our physical bodies. The carnal senses are necessary for human beings to live on earth; therefore, they are not to be viewed as evil or negative. The problem occurs when the carnal senses have been trained to provide inputs to the soul that antagonistically stand against the word of God. When this happens, the fleshly appetites and desires within all of us will begin to have preeminence over every aspect of our existence resulting in enslavement to the lusts and passions that permeate the fallen nature of man. This condition is addressed in Colossians 3 in the Bible which reveals the struggle that exists between carnality and obedience to Christ.

If then you were raised with Christ, seek those things which are above, where Christ is, sitting at the right hand of God. Set your mind on things above, not on things on the earth. For you died, and your life is hidden with Christ in God.
When Christ who is our life appears, then you also will appear with Him in glory. Therefore, put to death your members which are on the earth: fornication, uncleanness, passion, evil desire, and covetousness, which is idolatry. Because of these things the wrath of God is coming upon the sons of disobedience, in which you yourselves once walked when you lived in them. (Colossians 3:1-7)

We also find this condition addressed again in Galatians 5:16-21:

I say then: Walk in the Spirit, and you shall not fulfill the lust of the flesh. For the flesh lusts against the Spirit, and the Spirit against the flesh; and these are contrary to one another, so that you do not do the things that you wish. But if you are led by the Spirit, you are not under the law. Now the works of the flesh are evident, which are: adultery, fornication, uncleanness, lewdness, idolatry, sorcery, hatred, contentions, jealousies, outbursts of wrath, selfish ambitions, dissensions, heresies, envy, murders, drunkenness, revelries, and the like; of which I tell you beforehand, just as I also told you in time past, that those who practice such things will not inherit the kingdom of God.

As stated earlier in this chapter, we are dealing with the human soul that has been misaligned and altered resulting in a change of inner frequency that disallowed communication with God. This change of frequency is the result of the mind receiving signals from the world through the carnal senses at the expense of impulses received through the spirit inspired by the Holy Spirit. The carnalized mind described in Romans 8 is not "subject to the law of God, neither indeed can be";

therefore, those that are in the flesh (connected to the five carnal senses) are incapable of serving Jesus Christ and obeying the dictates of the Kingdom of God. This condition negates the ability to transmit information to God or receive information from God because the alienated state of the mind is not able to correspond with the spiritual world ruled by a holy and righteous God.

Satan's spirit continually inundates the senses with inspirations designed to motivate rebellion, sin, stubbornness, and insurrections against God's Kingdom; therefore, the scriptures command us to separate from these satanic inspirations to live holy lives that are pleasing to the Lord.

When Christians repent from sin, they willfully turn away from participating in Satan's sinful matrix, then they walk away from environmental influences that inspired the sin in the first place. The Bible does not instruct us to just believe the gospel, but we are instructed to first repent and *then* believe the gospel. Without sincere heartfelt repentance, the ability to believe the gospel is negated because the carnal mind is "not subject to the law of God, neither indeed can be." Right now, we are witnessing millions of professing Christians who have never become believers simply because they never really repented from the sinful lifestyles they have lived. As we saw in Chapter 3, Jesus gave very explicit instructions in Mark 1 concerning the salvation requirements when He stated the following:

Now after John was put in prison, Jesus came to Galilee, preaching the gospel of the kingdom of God, and saying, "The time is fulfilled, and the kingdom of God is at hand. Repent, and believe in the gospel." (Mark 1:14-15)

Sincere repentance begins the reprogramming process necessary to transform the mind repairing it from the damage done because of participation in the Satanic world systems. This reprogramming of the mind is what we call the process that matures a Christian making them able to receive inputs from the Kingdom of God, while simultaneously enabling individuals to transmit messages to God's throne. Once matured, Christians have an innate ability to live a righteous life because of the impartation of God's life that comes through His word and the blood of Jesus being applied to the soul. We will discuss this process further in chapter 5 as we examine spiritual maturity in the life of believers.

CHAPTER 5
Spiritual Maturity

Maturity is the quality of behaving mentally and emotionally like an adult or demonstrating a very advanced or developed form or state. Historically, there have been four main areas of human growth and development as it relates to maturation. These four areas are physical, mental, emotional, and spiritual growth. Each one of these areas develops and grows as individuals are exposed to situations, interactions, instructions, and circumstances that help to mold us into well-rounded, analytical adults. Physical maturity is the result of the normal development of the anatomical and biological features that all humans possess, while the other three areas of maturity are subject to variable inputs determined by environmental distinctions and inputs received from several different sources. The process, as described within the pages of this book, primarily deals with spiritual maturity which also impacts mental and emotional maturity. The mind and emotions are arenas of the soul that are impacted by the spirit; therefore, the effect of spiritual maturity can be evaluated by examining the mental development and emotional stability of an individual.

The word of God is the supernaturally inspired resource used by the Holy Spirit to nourish the human spirit causing it to grow into a mature child of God. God wants all of us to grow. Maturity is one of His purposes for our lives. In fact, Hebrews 6:1 tells us, “Let's press on to maturity” (CEB). God intends for us to always pursue spiritual growth so that we may “be conformed to the image of His Son” (Romans 8:29 ESV).

The Bible reveals to us in Hebrews 6 that normal spiritual growth in our lives culminates when we become conduits for the power of God. The writer of Hebrews is careful to warn us that maturity comes with a very heavy responsibility:

Therefore, leaving the discussion of the elementary principles of Christ, let us go on to perfection, not laying again the foundation of repentance from dead works and of faith toward God, of the doctrine of baptisms, of laying on of hands, of resurrection of the dead, and of eternal judgment. And this we will do if God permits. For it is impossible for those who were once enlightened, and have tasted the heavenly gift, and have become partakers of the Holy Spirit, and have tasted the good word of God and the powers of the age to come, if they fall away, to renew them again to repentance, since they crucify again for themselves the Son of God and put Him to an open shame. For the earth which drinks in the rain that often comes upon it, and bears herbs useful for those by whom it is cultivated, receives blessing from God; but if it bears thorns and briers, it is rejected and near to being cursed, whose end is to be burned. (Hebrews 6:1-8)

The phrase "elementary principles of Christ" informs us that growth is necessary to relate to the Lord as an obedient child. The scriptures indicate that the goal is "perfection," which is the Greek word *teleioteta*, which means maturity. As born-again Christians, the Bible refers to us as "babes in Christ" who need to grow up just like a physical newborn child.

Therefore, laying aside all malice, all deceit, hypocrisy, envy, and all evil speaking, as newborn babes, desire the pure milk of the word, that you may grow thereby, if indeed you have tasted that the Lord is gracious. (1 Peter 2:1-3)

None of us enter a relationship with the Lord fully mature and it takes time to develop into mature Christians that can understand God's mind and His way of conducting business. Just like babies fresh out of their mother's wombs, we need the time to grow and develop the wisdom necessary to live Christian lives before the world. When Christians are born again, it is imperative to remember that the spirit of man is reawakened from a deep sleep. The part of us that comes alive is surrounded by years of rebellious human tendencies that still need to be put to death. In fact, we all lived our lives feeding the monster that Satan used to lead us into all types of sinful behavior and depravity. After we come to the Lord, the process of restoration and transformation begins to realign our souls with the will of God and the principles of His Kingdom. Maturity is the goal that must be pursued because without it, none of us would be able to live the Christian life as prescribed by the Bible.

Flee also youthful lusts; but pursue righteousness, faith, love, peace with those who call on the Lord out of a pure heart. But avoid foolish and ignorant disputes, knowing that they generate strife. And a servant of the Lord must not quarrel but be gentle to all, able to teach, patient, in humility correcting those who are in opposition, if God perhaps will grant them repentance, so that they may know the truth, and that they may come to their senses and escape the snare of the devil, having been taken captive by him to do his will. (2 Timothy 2:22-26)

To better understand our spiritual development as Christians, we will look at the phases of human conception, gestation, and manifestation (birthing).

Conception

Physical conception occurs when a sperm cell joins to or fertilizes an egg cell. It is one of the four steps that happen to create a pregnancy. Spiritual conception occurs when the word of God interacts with the human spirit resulting in a child of God being conceived by the incorruptible seed of God's word. 1 Peter 1:22-25 tells us more about this process.

Since you have purified your souls in obeying the truth through the Spirit in sincere love of the brethren, love one another fervently with a pure heart, having been born again, not of corruptible seed but incorruptible, through the word of God which lives and abides forever, because "All flesh is as grass, and all the glory of man as the flower of the grass. The grass withers, and its flower falls away, but the word of the Lord endures forever." Now this is the word which by the gospel was preached to you.

The scriptures reveal to us that the word of God is the spiritual seed that God uses to conceive His nature within the spirit of the born-again Christian. Once conception takes place, the Holy Spirit begins the next progressive step of gestation to develop this newly conceived life into a mature child of God.

Gestation

Therefore, laying aside all malice, all deceit, hypocrisy, envy, and all evil speaking, as newborn babes, desire the pure milk of the word, that you may grow thereby, if indeed you have tasted that the Lord is gracious. (1 Peter 2:1-3)

Gestation is defined as the process or period of development inside the womb between conception and birth. Spiritual gestation takes place when the born-again spirit begins to grow as it feeds on the word of God. This process of growth will methodically begin to effect change within the soul of a Christian because God's eternal word is changing the way the soul operates. The nature of Christ forming in us changes our perception of the world, human appetites, natural desires, self-identity, emotions, thoughts, plans, and pursuits. As the Holy Spirit redirects the soul to feed on the word of God instead of inputs from the five carnal senses, Christians begin to change into individuals that reflect the principles of the Kingdom of God as opposed to the kingdom of Satan. The process of gestation takes time. As we submit our souls to "the process" ultimately the reality of the born-again experience will come alive inside of us and change our lives forever.

The Process

Manifestation

For I consider that the sufferings of this present time are not worthy to be compared with the glory which shall be revealed in us. For the earnest expectation of the creation eagerly waits for the revealing of the sons of God. For the creation was subjected to futility, not willingly, but because of Him who subjected it in hope; because the creation itself also will be delivered from the bondage of corruption into the glorious liberty of the children of God. For we know that the whole creation groans and labors with birth pangs together until now. Not only that, but we also have the first fruits of the Spirit, even we ourselves groan within ourselves, eagerly waiting for the adoption, the redemption of our body. For we were saved in this hope, but hope that is seen is not hope; for why does one still hope for what he sees? But if we hope for what we do not see, we eagerly wait for it with perseverance. (Romans 8:18-24)

Beloved, now are we the sons of God, and it doth not yet appear what we shall be: but we know that, when he shall appear, we shall be like him; for we shall see him as he is. (1 John 3:2)

The final phase of the maturation process occurs when the fully developed life is manifested to the world as a son of God. The word manifestation means an event, action, or object that clearly shows or embodies something, especially a theory or an abstract idea. When the process of internal development has reached its culmination, then the Holy Spirit displays the finished product to the world – a mature child of God. The mature child can be trusted to obey the promptings of God because the embedded nature willingly obeys the word of God.

It takes time to retrain the soul to be led by God's Holy Spirit. Most of us spent years in rebellion against God allowing our earthly, carnal appetites to lead us instead of the will of God as revealed through His word. The Bible tells us that there is an inner conflict between the carnal nature that receives from Satan's rebellious inspirations and the new nature that receives inspiration from God's Holy Spirit. Galatians 5 speaks on this inner conflict:

The Process

I say then: Walk in the Spirit, and you shall not fulfill the lust of the flesh. For the flesh lusts against the Spirit, and the Spirit against the flesh; and these are contrary to one another, so that you do not do the things that you wish. But if you are led by the Spirit, you are not under the law. (Galatians 5:16-18)

This inner conflict will never go away as long as we live on this earth inside of these temporal flesh and blood bodies with our five carnal senses activated. Because of this, the allure of the world and the sin contained therein still have a magnetic drawing power that seeks to tempt us to participate in Satan's amusement park. The born-again Christian has experienced a regeneration of the spirit that allows us to overcome these temptations as we yield ourselves to the power of God and His Holy Spirit. The word of God is provided to feed the appetite of the new man, birthed inside of us when we receive Jesus Christ as our Savior. If we willfully stay in the process of regeneration, God is committed to keeping us and protecting us from Satan's infiltrations. This is the reason Galatians 5 states, "But if you are led by the Spirit, you are not under the law." Every Christian must exercise the God-given ability to choose to walk in obedience every day because the Lord will keep everyone who desires to be kept. Let's look at what the Apostle Paul has to say about this.

Do you not know that those who run in a race all run, but one receives the prize? Run in such a way that you may obtain it. And everyone who competes for the prize is temperate in all things. Now they do it to obtain a perishable crown, but we for an imperishable crown. Therefore, I run thus: not with uncertainty. Thus, I fight not as one who beats the air. But I discipline my body and bring it into subjection, lest, when I have preached to others, I should become disqualified.
(1 Corinthians 9:24-27)

Yes, indeed friends, spiritual maturity is the goal of transformation, and we all must stay committed to the process to achieve the purpose that God has planned for our lives. God has done His part by sending His Son to die for our sins releasing us from the penalties associated with rebellion. We must do our part by remaining faithfully committed within the confines of the word of God and not allowing Satan to tempt us back into rebellion again. Mature Christians have committed themselves to live in obedience to the laws of God's Kingdom and the Holy Spirit is committed to lead us home because we remain faithful. In chapter 6, we will take a closer look at the process used by God's Holy Spirit to keep us on track in our progression into eternal life.

CHAPTER 6
A Life Giving Spirit

So also, is the resurrection of the dead. The body is sown in corruption, it is raised in incorruption. It is sown in dishonor; it is raised in glory. It is sown in weakness; it is raised in power. It is sown as a natural body; it is raised a spiritual body. There is a natural body, and there is a spiritual body. And so, it is written, "The first man Adam became a living being." The last Adam became a life-giving spirit. (1 Corinthians 15:42-45)

Here the scriptures reveal to us that Jesus Christ, as the last Adam, became a life-giving spirit after His resurrection from the dead. God has initiated a program that is designed to lead us into the reality of eternal life, but His systemic design only functions as Christians are willing to relinquish their hold on temporal, earthly existence. Embedded in all of us is an innate desire to live healthy, prosperous, enjoyable lives here on earth, if we were allowed to make this world our home. There is absolutely nothing wrong with living a good life here, but the problem arises when this life is elevated over and above the life that we receive from Jesus Christ when we are born-again. Christians must understand that the primary purpose of salvation is not to enjoy this present world by seeking to have your best life now because sooner or later, we all must die. This world will become unimportant as eternity becomes our new home. Frankly, when one compares temporal life with eternal life, it becomes obvious that a few years here are inconsequential and meaningless when a timeless life is brought into focus.

God knows that we all need time to make this adjustment and He has provided the Holy Spirit to lead us into eternal life. He has also given us tools to help this process along. In this chapter, we will look at four tools available to Christians which are designed to keep us focused on the transition from life on earth to life in heaven. If we remain faithfully committed to God's word and His Kingdom principles, the Holy Spirit will lead and guide us home. But, commitment to the process is necessary and time must be spent every day adhering to God's spiritual curriculum. The four tools provided to us by God to help us advance and grow are the word of God, prayer, fasting, and praise and worship.

The Word of God

In the beginning was the Word, and the Word was with God, and the Word was God. He was in the beginning with God. All things were made through Him, and without Him nothing was made that was made. In Him was life, and the life was the light of men. And the light shines in the darkness, and the darkness did not comprehend it. (John 1:1-5)

If you abide in Me, and My words abide in you, you will ask what you desire, and it shall be done for you. By this My Father is glorified, that you bear much fruit; so, you will be My disciples. "As the Father loved Me, I also have loved you; abide in My love. (John 15:17-19)

Thy word is a lamp unto my feet, and a light unto my path. (Psalm 119:105)

Your word I have hidden in my heart, that I might not sin against You! (Psalm 119:11)

The Process

These scriptures, along with many others, stress the importance of making the word of God the central focus of your Christian experience. As you read this book, it becomes very apparent that everything that is written here consistently refers to the word of God as the primary source for our Christian lives. God's word is multifaceted and must be understood based on the illumination provided by the Bible. Christians must understand that references to the "word" of God have different definitions and transmit different ideas based on the context, original language, and focus of the text. For example, John 1:1-5 must be understood based on the original text and the idea that is transmitted in these verses. Let's take a closer look to get the full revelation of these scriptures. The first sentence states that "in the beginning was the Word, and the Word was with God, and the Word was God." The word translated "Word" here is the Greek word *logos* which refers to the use of evidence and reasoning to persuasively support a claim. The scriptures state that the "Logos" was with God and the "Logos" was God; therefore, we can conclude that the Word of God is the divine intellect and reasoning capabilities of God.

This divine intellect was embodied in the man we know historically as Jesus Christ. Later in John 1:14, the scripture reveals that "the Word was made flesh, and dwelt among us, (and we beheld His glory, the glory as of the only begotten of the Father,) full of grace and truth." The word of God is the focal point for everything pertaining to a Christian's growth and development and it must be at the center of our relationship with the Lord. The Bible emphasizes this when it states:

Study to show thyself approved unto God, a workman that does not need to be ashamed, rightly dividing the word of truth. (2 Timothy 2:15)

The most important tool available to us is the transformative power contained within the pages of the Bible and every born-again believer is commanded to consistently study the scriptures in order to mature and be approved by the Holy Spirit.

Prayer

The Process

Then He spoke a parable to them, that men always ought to pray and not lose heart, saying: "There was in a certain city a judge who did not fear God nor regard man. Now there was a widow in that city; and she came to him, saying, 'Get justice for me from my adversary." And he would not for a while; but afterward he said within himself, "Though I do not fear God nor regard man, yet because this widow troubles me I will avenge her, lest by her continual coming she weary me." Then the Lord said, "Hear what the unjust judge said. And shall God not avenge His own elect who cry out day and night to Him, though He bears long with them? I tell you that He will avenge them speedily. Nevertheless, when the Son of Man comes, will He really find faith on the earth?" (Luke 18:1-8)

Rejoice always, pray without ceasing, in everything give thanks; for this is the will of God in Christ Jesus for you. Do not quench the Spirit. (1 Thessalonians 5:16-19)

Praying always with all prayer and supplication in the Spirit, being watchful to this end with all perseverance and supplication for all the saints— and for me, that utterance may be given to me, that I may open my mouth boldly to make known the mystery of the gospel, for which I am an ambassador in chains; that in it I may speak boldly, as I ought to speak. (Ephesians 6:18-20)

Now it came to pass, as He was praying in a certain place, when He ceased, that one of His disciples said to Him, "Lord, teach us to pray, as John also taught his disciples." So He said to them, "When you pray, say: Our Father in heaven, Hallowed be Your name. Your kingdom comes. Your will be done on earth as it is in heaven. Give us day by day our daily bread. And forgive us our sins, for we also forgive everyone who is indebted to us. And do not lead us into temptation but deliver us from the evil one." (Luke 11:1-4)

As these scriptures reveal, the second most important tool we need in the process is a disciplined prayer life. It is imperative that every believer cultivates a consistent prayer life to develop a relationship with the Lord based on intimacy and continual fellowship. We all get to know people when we spend time talking and communicating with them and getting to know the Lord is no different. It is very important that every Christian takes time to pray every day. Keeping a journal of prayer and answers to prayer will help you document what was prayed and how and when God answered your prayers. Learn to pray very specific prayers asking the Lord for His direction, His instructions, His desires, and His will for your life. This is one of the most important aspects of your Christian experience that tends to speed up conversion and transformation within the inner man. No matter what happens in your life, keep praying!

Fasting

Is this not the fast that I have chosen: to lose the bonds of wickedness, to undo the heavy burdens, to let the oppressed go free, and that you break every yoke? Is it not to share your bread with the hungry, and that you bring to your house the poor who are cast out; when you see the naked, that you cover him, and not hide yourself from your own flesh? Then your light shall break forth like the morning, your healing shall spring forth speedily, and your righteousness shall go before you; the glory of the Lord shall be your rear guard.

Then you shall call, and the Lord will answer; you shall cry, and He will say, "Here I am." If you take away the yoke from your midst, the pointing of the finger, and speaking wickedness, if you extend your soul to the hungry and satisfy the afflicted soul, then your light shall dawn in the darkness, and your darkness shall be as the noonday. The Lord will guide you continually, and satisfy your soul in drought, and strengthen your bones; you shall be like a watered garden, and like a spring of water, whose waters do not fail. Those from among you shall build the old waste places; you shall raise up the foundations of many generations; and you shall be called the Repairer of the Breach, The Restorer of Streets to Dwell In. (Isaiah 58:6-12)

Then the disciples of John came to Him, saying, "Why do we and the Pharisees fast often, but Your disciples do not fast?" And Jesus said to them, "Can the friends of the bridegroom mourn if the bridegroom is with them? But the days will come when the bridegroom will be taken away from them, and then they will fast. No one puts a piece of unshrunk cloth on an old garment;

for the patch pulls away from the garment, and the tear is made worse. Nor do they put new wine into old wineskins, or else the wineskins break, the wine is spilled, and the wineskins are ruined. But they put new wine into new wineskins, and both are preserved." (Matthew 9:14-17)

The third important tool necessary to enhance the process is fasting. Fasting is an important part of the Christian experience because it focuses the souls of born-again believers on spiritual things in direct opposition to the things that are in the world. When we set aside time to fast, spiritual senses are sharpened and the word of God becomes extremely clear as sensual things diminish in their intensity. Most people believe that fasting only requires not eating food, but an acceptable fast incorporates the denial of all five carnal senses which serves to heighten the awareness of spiritual senses; therefore, all five senses are required to be denied including sight, sound, smell, touch, and taste. All Christians must dedicate time to fasting and prayer to help them mature and advance in the Kingdom of God.

Praise and Worship

Therefore, do not be unwise, but understand what the will of the Lord is, and do not be drunk with wine, in which is dissipation; but be filled with the Spirit, speaking to one another in psalms and hymns and spiritual songs, singing and making melody in your heart to the Lord, giving thanks always for all things to God the Father in the name of our Lord Jesus Christ, submitting to one another in the fear of God. (Ephesians 5:17-21)

Teach and counsel each other with all the wisdom he gives. Sing psalms and hymns and spiritual songs to God with thankful hearts. And whatever you do or say, do it as a representative of the Lord Jesus, giving thanks through him to God the Father. (Colossians 3:16-17)

Praise the Lord! Praise God in His sanctuary; praise Him in His mighty firmament! Praise Him for His mighty acts; praise Him according to His excellent greatness! Praise Him with the sound of the trumpet; praise Him with the lute and harp! Praise Him with the timbrel and dance; praise Him with stringed instruments and flutes! Praise Him with loud cymbals; praise Him with clashing cymbals! Let everything that has breath praise the Lord. Praise the Lord! (Psalm 150:1-6)

The last tool in the process is praise and worship, which lifts up the human spirit and soul before the throne of God as we glorify the Lord with our voices and our hearts. Praise and worship invite the presence of the Lord to abide with us because the Bible informs us that "God inhabits the praises of His people."(Psalm 22:3) A soul that is filled with the praises of God has an atmosphere conducive to receiving revelation, inspiration, and guidance from the Holy Spirit. In that environment, the soul is easily converted and transformed in order to be led by the Spirit of God. Music invites spiritual elements from both the Kingdom of God and the kingdom of darkness to draw nearer to those involved in worship. It is extremely important that Christians continually praise the Lord as David stated, "I will bless the LORD at all times: his praise shall continually be in my mouth." (Psalm 34:1)

These four tools are designed to speed up the conversion process by focusing the hearts and minds of Christians on the Kingdom of God at the expense of this present evil world. Every born-again believer needs to actively engage in the process of change every day, especially as we draw closer to the end of the age. I admonish you to embrace these four spiritual tools and soon you'll find yourself methodically metamorphosizing from a caterpillar into a butterfly. Praise the Lord!

CHAPTER 7
Enemies of the Process

In this chapter, we introduce you to three enemies of the process that are always present attempting to undermine your progression and growth in the Kingdom of God. Although there are multitudes of weapons designed by Satan to stop your growth and maturity, we will focus on three of the most powerful tools designed to delay, restrict, or prevent the transformation of Christians.

The World

Do not love the world or the things in the world. If anyone loves the world, the love of the Father is not in him. For all that is in the world—the lust of the flesh, the lust of the eyes, and the pride of life—is not of the Father but is of the world. And the world is passing away, and the lust of it; but he who does the will of God abides forever. (1 John 2:15-17)

Grace to you and peace from God the Father and our Lord Jesus Christ, who gave Himself for our sins, that

He might deliver us from this present evil age, according to the will of our God and Father, to whom be glory forever and ever. Amen. (Galatians 1:3-5)

But if our gospel is hidden, it is hid to them that are lost: In whom the god of this world hath blinded the minds of them which believe not, lest the light of the glorious gospel of Christ, who is the image of God, should shine unto them. (2 Corinthians 4:3-4)

One of the most powerful enemies that confronts a Christian's spiritual development is the world. What exactly is "the world"? We first have to define the two words used in the New Testament when the Bible speaks of the domain known as "the world". The first word is the Greek word *cosmos* which refers to the fashions and elements contained within the physical world. We get English words like cosmetics and cosmopolitan from this word and usually these words describe decorations or the alluring elements associated with earthly existence. The other word translated as "world" in the Bible is the Greek word *aeon* which refers to the time and space continuum that houses the elements found in the cosmos. To get a full understanding of the word "world" it is important to combine both definitions. The biblical understanding of this word is simply the elements contained within the confines of time and space. The Bible instructs us in 1 John 2 not to "love the things of the world" because these things are temporary. When Christians get enthralled with the bright, shiny objects found here, it is easy to be drawn away from God's plan for our lives and His eternal will. We all have to guard ourselves against becoming enamored with the attractions and novelties that Satan uses to keep us entertained and distracted away from the Lord's word and His presence. Indeed, the world is a powerful enemy that must be addressed as Christians embrace the transformational process.

The Flesh

There is therefore now no condemnation to them which are in Christ Jesus, who walk not after the flesh, but after the Spirit. For the law of the Spirit of life in Christ Jesus hath made me free from the law of sin and death. For what the law could not do, in that it was weak through the flesh, God sending his own Son in the likeness of sinful flesh, and for sin, condemned sin in the flesh: that the righteousness of the law might be fulfilled in us, who walk not after the flesh, but after the Spirit. For they that are after the flesh do mind the things of the flesh; but they that are after the Spirit the things of the Spirit. For to be carnally minded is death; but to be spiritually minded is life and peace. Because the carnal mind is enmity against God: for it is not subject to the law of God, neither indeed can be. So, then they that are in the flesh cannot please God. (Romans 8:1-8)

But the natural man receives not the things of the Spirit of God: for they are foolishness unto him: neither can he know them, because they are spiritually discerned. But he that is spiritual judges all things, yet he himself is judged of no man. (1 Corinthians 2:14-15)

Now the works of the flesh are manifest, which are these; Adultery, fornication, uncleanness, lasciviousness, idolatry, witchcraft, hatred, variance, emulations, wrath, strife, seditions, heresies, envying, murders, drunkenness, reveling, and such like: of the which I tell you before, as I have also told you in time past, that they which do such things shall not inherit the kingdom of God. But the fruit of the Spirit is love, joy, peace, longsuffering, gentleness, goodness, faith, meekness, temperance: against such there is no law. And they that are Christ's have crucified the flesh with the affections and lusts. If we live in the Spirit, let us also walk in the Spirit. Let us not be desirous of vain glory, provoking one another, envying one another. (Galatians 5:19-26)

The second enemy of the process is the flesh. The flesh is defined as the fallen human nature inherited from our father Adam. The Bible has several terms that refer to this fallen nature and all of them describe negative human personality traits that negate fruitfulness in the Kingdom of God. In scriptures, the flesh is called soulish, carnal, natural, and most often just "the flesh". The flesh is the unregenerated, unchanged sinful nature that imprints the soul when we are born, and it has a natural inclination to append itself to this world and the things contained therein.

This is why we must all be born again in order to begin

the process of mortifying or killing the old Adamic nature that has imprisoned us our entire lives. This "natural man," as 1 Corinthians 2 calls it, seeks to undermine our growth when we are saved by intruding into our minds and emotions with all the distracting elements contained in the world. Make no mistake about it friends, the flesh is evil, and it must be conquered to serve God and live fruitful lives in His Kingdom. The flesh is chained to the will of Satan and bound to his kingdom. Ephesians 2 makes this clear:

And you hath he quickened, who were dead in trespasses and sins; wherein in time past ye walked according to the course of this world, according to the prince of the power of the air, the spirit that now works in the children of disobedience: among whom also we all had our conversation in times past in the lusts of our flesh, fulfilling the desires of the flesh and of the mind; and were by nature the children of wrath, even as others. (Ephesians 2:1-3)

The nature of the flesh is very sinister, and it must be resisted and put to death to serve the Lord. The fallen human nature is not subject to God's law and internally it will fight the regenerated, born-again spirit housed within Christians. It is imperative that we all acknowledge this and become equipped to war against this inner enemy that attempts to hinder our progression. The flesh is a formidable foe, but Jesus Christ defeated it on the cross and the process is necessary to help enforce His victory. So, get your Christian armor on and take possession of your mind, your thoughts, your emotions, and your feelings for the glory of God.

The Devil

How you have fallen from heaven, O Lucifer, son of the morning! How you are cut down to the ground, you who weakened the nations! For you have said in your heart: 'I will ascend into heaven, I will exalt my throne above the stars of God; I will also sit on the mount of the congregation on the farthest sides of the north; I will ascend above the heights of the clouds, I will be like the Highest.' Yet you shall be brought down to Hell, To the lowest depths of the Pit. (Isaiah 14:12-15)

But if our gospel is hidden, it is hidden to them that are lost: In whom the god of this world hath blinded the minds of them which believe not, lest the light of the glorious gospel of Christ, who is the image of God, should shine unto them. (2 Corinthians 4:3-4)

I will no longer talk much with you, for the ruler of this world is coming, and he has nothing in Me. But that the world may know that I love the Father, and as the Father gave Me commandment, so I do. Arise, let us go from here. (John 14:30-31)

The last enemy we will address here is the person orchestrating all the circumstances that attempt to divert Christians away from maturation and viability in God's Kingdom. Satan is the individual committed to stopping the children of God from reaching their full potential in the Lord and he works tirelessly to implement strategies and tactics dedicated to this purpose. The Bible refers to Satan as the god of this world, the ruler of this world, the prince of the power of the air, and the spirit that now works in the children of rebellion. Plainly stated, Satan is an evil character that exists only to steal, kill, and destroy human beings and he enjoys tormenting us whenever and wherever he can.

The two names the Bible calls this evil entity are “Satan” and “the Devil”. As Satan he manifests himself as “the adversary” and as the Devil he is revealed as “an accuser”. These two titles give us insight into his daily activities: namely, spending all day resisting us and accusing us before the throne of God. He is the spiritual presence that controls the world trying to tempt our fleshly natures to join him in his insurrection against God. He has had thousands of years to perfect his war plans and human beings are no match for his attacks outside of a relationship with the Lord Jesus Christ. The Bible tells us that when the smoke clears and the battles of this life come to an end, Satan will be sent to a lake of fire forever. In the meantime, Christians must resist him daily by submitting to God and remaining separated from Satan's spheres of influence. Yes, the process is real, but enemies of this process are all around us to prevent our success and progression; therefore, it is imperative to stay focused and committed to daily disciplines designed to make sure that we become victorious overcomers in the army of Jesus Christ.

Hopefully, this book is helping you to become more aware of these enemies while providing tools to enhance your ability to win in every area of life.

CHAPTER 8
Moses the Metamorphosized Man

In this chapter, we are going to do a short case study of a man who went through the process of metamorphosis to be used by God as a leader and commander of the armies of God. The life of Moses illustrates how God prepares an individual for service and exactly what must be done to make sure our efforts are productive and not in vain. The Bible introduces us to Moses in the Book of Exodus where it states:

And the midwives said to Pharaoh, "Because the Hebrew women are not like the Egyptian women; for they are lively and give birth before the midwives come to them." Therefore, God dealt well with the midwives, and the people multiplied and grew very mighty. And so it was, because the midwives feared God, that He provided households for them. So, Pharaoh commanded all his people, saying, "Every son who is born you shall cast into the river, and every daughter you shall save alive." (Exodus 1:19-22)

And a man of the house of Levi went and took as wife a daughter of Levi. So, the woman conceived and bore a son. And when she saw that he was a beautiful child, she hid him for three months. But when she could no longer hide him, she made a vessel of bulrushes for him, daubed it with asphalt and pitch, put the child in it, and laid it in the reeds by the river's bank. And his sister stood afar off, to know what would be done to him. (Exodus 2:1-4)

These two passages of scripture found in Exodus chapters 1 and 2 reveal to us the circumstances of Moses' birth. The Israelites were slaves in Egypt when Moses was born, and Pharaoh was attempting to limit the number of male children born because he feared that they would grow to outnumber the Egyptians. Pharaoh commanded the midwives who delivered the babies to kill all the male children and let the female children live. This is the background concerning the birth of Moses and now we'll see how Moses ended up in Pharaoh's palace.

Then the daughter of Pharaoh came down to bathe at

the river. And her maidens walked along the riverside; and when she saw the ark among the reeds, she sent her maid to get it. And when she opened it, she saw the child, and behold, the baby wept. So, she had compassion on him, and said, "This is one of the Hebrews' children." Then his sister said to Pharaoh's daughter, "Shall I go and call a nurse for you from the Hebrew women, that she may nurse the child for you?" And Pharaoh's daughter said to her, "Go." So, the maiden went and called the child's mother. Then Pharaoh's daughter said to her, "Take this child away and nurse him for me, and I will give you your wages." So, the woman took the child and nursed him. And the child grew, and she brought him to Pharaoh's daughter, and he became her son. So, she called his name Moses, saying, "Because I drew him out of the water." (Exodus 2:5-10)

These scriptures reveal how Moses ended up in Egypt and was raised as the son of Pharaoh's daughter. In fact, Moses became so favored by Pharaoh, that he was thought to be next in line to the throne. However, the rest of the passages found in Exodus 2 tell the story of how Moses ended up leaving Egypt, rejected by Pharaoh because he found out that Moses was a Hebrew and not an Egyptian. Moses lived 40 years in Egypt and ended up in the desert tending flocks of sheep. He lived as a shepherd for 40 more years and eventually, God came to him commanding him to return to Egypt to set the people of God free from 400 years of slavery.

Now Moses was tending the flock of Jethro his father-in-law, the priest of Midian. And he led the flock to the back of the desert, and came to Horeb, the mountain of God. And the Angel of the Lord appeared to him in a flame of fire from the midst of a bush. So, he looked, and behold, the bush was burning with fire, but the bush was not consumed. Then Moses said, "I will now turn aside and see this great sight, why the bush does not burn" So. When the Lord saw that he turned aside to look, God called to him from the midst of the bush and said, "Moses, Moses!" And he said, "Here I am." Then He said, "Do not draw near this place. Take your sandals off your feet, for the place where you stand is holy ground." Moreover, He said, "I am the God of your father—the God of Abraham, the God of Isaac, and the God of Jacob." And Moses hid his face, for he was afraid to look upon God. And the Lord said: "I have surely seen the oppression of My people who are in Egypt, and have heard their cry because of their taskmasters, for I know their sorrows. So, I have come down to deliver them out of the hand of the Egyptians, and to bring them up from that land to a good and large land, to a land flowing with milk and honey, to the place of the Canaanites and the Hittites and the Amorites and the Perizzites and the Hivites and the Jebusites. Now therefore, behold, the cry of the children of Israel has come to Me, and I have also seen the oppression with which the Egyptians oppress them. Come now, therefore, and I will send you to Pharaoh that you may bring My people, the children of Israel, out of Egypt." (Exodus 3:1-10)

The Lord called Moses out of the wilderness inspiring him to return to Egypt as the leader of the tribes of Israel. He led the Israelites out of captivity into the wilderness where they spent 40 years wandering in a circle without reaching their destination. God used the wilderness experience to purge the damage done to the minds of the Israelites because of slavery and He also used the experience to teach His people how to conduct warfare against the adversaries they would face in the future. Moses never reached the Promised Land that God was giving to Abraham's descendants, but he led them right up to the edge of the land where he died after 40 years of leadership.

So, Moses the servant of the Lord died there in the land of Moab, according to the word of the Lord. And He buried him in a valley in the land of Moab, opposite Beth Peor; but no one knows his grave to this day. Moses was one hundred and twenty years old when he died. His eyes were not dim, nor his natural vigor diminished. And the children of Israel wept for Moses in the plains of Moab thirty days. So, the days of weeping and mourning for Moses ended. (Deuteronomy 34:5-8)

Moses died when he was 120 years old; therefore, we can ascertain that Moses lived in Egypt for 40 years, he was sent away to the desert as a shepherd for 40 years and he led the tribes of Israel for 40 years. Moses' life was dissected into the three necessary parts to make him a useful tool in the hands of God and achieve His purposes. Moses was raised in Egypt for 40 years where he was programmed to think like an Egyptian and taught to worship the false gods of the Egyptians. God sent him to the wilderness for 40 years to wash the Egyptian nature out of his soul preparing him to be a vessel that was able to be used by the Lord to accomplish His will. For the final 40 years, Moses was ordained to lead the children of Israel out of captivity and into freedom towards the Promised Land because his reprogrammed soul was able to interact with God by hearing His voice and obeying His instructions. Basically, Moses is the perfect example of a man that went through the process of metamorphosis changing him from an Egyptian into a servant of God.

This three-step process is the same journey that Christians go through. We begin our lives in the world (Egypt) then we are born again to begin the process of sanctification or cleaning the soul (Wilderness). Last, we arrive at our final destination, which is obedient interaction with Jesus Christ as our Lord and Savior (Promised Land). This cursory examination of Moses provides insight into how God deals with all of us to clear the leftover debris from the world housed in our souls. Each of us must realize that being born again is not an instantaneous change, but it is a process that we go through designed to change us and teach us the ways of God. We should learn to embrace what God is doing and be willing to respond as He initiates His mysterious plan within each of us. The process of transformation is necessary, and the transformation of the mind opens new dimensions of revelation and participation in the Kingdom of God. It is time for the Church to move away from wilderness living to experience the fruitfulness found in the Promised Land.

CHAPTER 9
The Celestial Church on Earth

Therefore, leaving the discussion of the elementary principles of Christ, let us go on to perfection, not laying again the foundation of repentance from dead works and of faith toward God, of the doctrine of baptisms, of laying on of hands, of resurrection of the dead, and of eternal judgment. And this we will do if God permits. For it is impossible for those who were once enlightened, and have tasted the heavenly gift, and have become partakers of the Holy Spirit, and have tasted the good word of God and the powers of the age to come, if they fall away, to renew them again to repentance, since they crucify again for themselves the Son of God and put Him to an open shame. (Hebrews 6:1-6)

Now concerning spiritual gifts, brethren, I do not want you to be ignorant: You know that you were Gentiles, carried away to these dumb idols, however you were led. Therefore, I make known to you that no one speaking by the Spirit of God calls Jesus accursed, and no one can say that Jesus is Lord except by the Holy Spirit. There are diversities of gifts, but the same Spirit. There are differences of ministries, but the same Lord. And there are diversities of activities, but it is the same God who works all in all. But the manifestation of the Spirit is given to each one for the profit of all: for to one is given the word of wisdom through the Spirit, to another the word of knowledge through the same Spirit, to another faith by the same Spirit, to another gifts of healings by the same Spirit, to another the working of miracles, to another prophecy, to another discerning of spirits, to another different kinds of tongues, to another the interpretation of tongues. But one and the same Spirit works all these things, distributing to each one individually as He wills. (1 Corinthians 12:1-11)

And He said to them, "Go into all the world and preach the gospel to every creature. He who believes and is baptized will be saved; but he who does not believe will be condemned. And these signs will follow those who believe: In My name they will cast out demons; they will speak with new tongues; they will take up serpents; and if they drink anything deadly, it will by no means hurt

them; they will lay hands on the sick, and they will recover." So then, after the Lord had spoken to them, He was received up into heaven, and sat down at the right hand of God. And they went out and preached everywhere, the Lord working with them and confirming the word through the accompanying signs. Amen.
(Mark 16:15-20)

Now we find that the Bible provides insight into what Christians should look like once the process of transformation is complete. Christianity is not designed to make individuals into members of churches because church membership has no benefit to lost souls that still need Jesus Christ as Savior. The primary purpose of salvation is to reconnect born-again believers with God through His Son, the Lord Jesus Christ. When Christians are reconnected to God, we experience a rebirthing of our spirits through organic conception that parallels the birthing of a human child.

Since you have purified your souls in obeying the truth through the Spirit in sincere love of the brethren, love one another fervently with a pure heart, having been born again, not of corruptible seed but incorruptible, through the word of God which lives and abides forever, because all flesh is as grass, and all the glory of man as the flower of the grass. The grass withers, and its flower falls away, but the word of the Lord endures forever. Now this is the word which by the gospel was preached to you. (1 Peter 1:22-25)

When Jesus knew in Himself that His disciples complained about this, He said to them, "Does this offend you? What then if you should see the Son of Man ascend where He was before? It is the Spirit who gives life; the flesh profits nothing. The words that I speak to you are spirit, and they are life. But there are some of you who do not believe." For Jesus knew from the beginning who they were who did not believe, and who would betray Him. And He said, "Therefore I have said to you that no one can come to Me unless it has been granted to him by My Father." From that time many of His disciples went back and walked with Him no more. (John 6:61-66)

The only people capable of living the Christian life are

those who have been conceived by the eternal word of God which unifies with the human spirit causing it to come alive again. The word of God in written and spoken form has the power to impart incorruptible seed into our spirits which is able to generate eternal life. This impartation of the word is necessary to begin the process that transforms the soul and renews the mind as the seed of the word gestates and grows a new nature within us.

Therefore, from now on, we regard no one according to the flesh. Even though we have known Christ according to the flesh, yet now we know Him thus no longer. Therefore, if anyone is in Christ, he is a new creation; old things have passed away; behold, all things have become new. (2 Corinthians 5:16-17)

Once conceived, the new spiritual man is surrounded by a soul and body that has most often spent years in sin. Therefore, it is necessary to refabricate the house that the new spiritual man lives in transforming it into a place suitable for a child of God. The Book of Timothy speaks to this as Paul informs young Timothy that he must become a vessel fit for the Master to use:

Nevertheless, the solid foundation of God stands, having this seal: "The Lord knows those who are His," and, "Let everyone who names the name of Christ depart from iniquity." But in a great house there are not only vessels of gold and silver, but also of wood and clay, some for honor and some for dishonor.

Therefore, if anyone cleanses himself from the latter, he will be a vessel for honor, sanctified and useful for the Master, prepared for every good work. (2 Timothy 2:19-21)

The mystery of the gospel reveals to us that God has determined to have a faithful family of believers that will display His Kingdom on the earth to those who are seeking freedom from Satan's insidious prison planet. The Celestial Church on Earth is made up of citizens who have the attributes of heavenly beings while living within the limited confines of flesh and blood bodies. The process becomes necessary to renovate earthly bodies so they can accommodate the celestial spirits contained inside the human form. To accomplish this, born-again Christians are instructed to undergo a process called "the renewing of the mind" as described

The Process
in Romans 12 and Ephesians 4:

I beseech you therefore, brethren, by the mercies of God, that you present your bodies a living sacrifice, holy, acceptable to God, which is your reasonable service. And do not be conformed to this world, but be transformed by the renewing of your mind, that you may prove what is that good and acceptable and perfect will of God. (Romans 12:1-2)

This I say, therefore, and testify in the Lord, that you should no longer walk as the rest of the Gentiles walk, in the futility of their mind, having their understanding darkened, being alienated from the life of God, because of the ignorance that is in them, because of the blindness of their heart; who, being past feeling, have given themselves over to lewdness, to work all uncleanness with greediness. But you have not so learned Christ, if indeed you have heard Him and have been taught by Him, as the truth is in Jesus: that you put off, concerning your former conduct, the old man which grows corrupt according to the deceitful lusts, and be renewed in the spirit of your mind, and that you put on the new man which was created according to God, in true righteousness and holiness. (Ephesians 4:17-24)

Although most of us have been taught the word of God systematically over the years, the mind is an area that has been somewhat neglected in gospel presentations. This area must be addressed in order for us to progress further into a deeper revelation of Jesus Christ. In fact, after salvation, the renewing of the mind is the most important aspect of our maturation and growth.

Organic growth always requires the expansion of the organism that is undergoing growth; therefore, the born-again spirit must expand its influence into every aspect of our lives to be productive. It is imperative that Christians understand the design of each facet of human existence; namely, the body, soul, and spirit. Now we will look at these three distinct areas of human existence along with their prevailing character traits.

Body

The dictionary defines the body as the physical structure and material substance of an animal or plant, living or dead. The Bible usually refers to the body as flesh and blood and the scriptures clearly state that "flesh and blood cannot inherit the kingdom of God; neither doth corruption inherit incorruption." (1 Corinthians 15:50) The Bible also describes the main purpose for the body when it states:

All things are lawful for me, but all things are not helpful. All things are lawful for me, but I will not be brought under the power of any. Foods for the stomach and the stomach for foods, but God will destroy both it and them. Now the body is not for sexual immorality but for the Lord, and the Lord for the body. And God both raised up the Lord and will also raise us up by His power. Do you not know that your bodies are members of Christ? Shall I then take the members of Christ and make them members of a harlot? Certainly not! Or do you not know that he who is joined to a harlot is one body with her? For "the two," He says, "shall become one flesh." But he who is joined to the Lord is one spirit with Him. Flee sexual immorality. Every sin that a man does is outside the body, but he who commits sexual immorality sins against his own body. Or do you not know that your body is the temple of the Holy Spirit who is in you, whom you have from God, and you are not your own? For you were bought at a price; therefore, glorify God in your body and in your spirit, which are God's. (1 Corinthians 6:12-20)

Our bodies are provided as vessels for the Lord to express Himself through as we give them back to Him to use for His divine purposes. Sin centers around the fact that we took the Lord's body from Him and used it to enjoy the sensations of pleasure that come through the five carnal senses (hearing, seeing, tasting, touching, and smelling). Satan has devised many ways to assault the five senses through temptations that are designed to draw our bodies into these pleasurable (sinful) activities. This is the reason why the Bible instructs us to run from sexual sin because of the extreme pleasure that fornication initiates within the body. Sexual sin can stimulate all five senses simultaneously, making the act of sexual intercourse a nuclear bomb in the devil's arsenal of weapons. After we are born-again, the Bible instructs Christians in Romans 12:1 to present our bodies back to God which is our "reasonable service." When we return the Lord's stolen body back to Him, the process of restoring the soul begins.

Soul

In the New Testament, the Greek word traditionally translated "soul" is *psyche.* In the Greek scriptures *psyche* is used to translate each instance of the Hebrew word for breath (*nephesh*) and substantially has the same meaning – the rational and immortal soul.
to the inner man housed within the body consisting of the mind, the will, the emotions, and conscious awareness.

These things we also speak, not in words which man's wisdom teaches but which the Holy Spirit teaches, comparing spiritual things with spiritual. But the NATURAL man does not receive the things of the Spirit of God, for they are foolishness to him; nor can he know them, because they are spiritually discerned. But he who is spiritual judges all things, yet he himself is rightly judged by no one. For "who has known the mind of the Lord that he may instruct Him?" But we have the mind of Christ." (1 Corinthians 2:13-16)

For those who live according to the FLESH set their

minds on the things of the FLESH, but those who live according to the Spirit, the things of the Spirit. For to be CARNALLY minded is death, but to be spiritually minded is life and peace.
Because the CARNAL mind is enmity against God; for it is not subject to the law of God, nor indeed can be. So then, those who are in the FLESH cannot please God. (Romans 8:5-8)

For the FLESH lusts against the Spirit, and the Spirit against the FLESH; and these are contrary to one another, so that you do not do the things that you wish. (Galatians 5:17)

Emphasis added.

After salvation, this is the insidious battle that rages within the confines of the human soul as Satan attempts to draw Christians back into the life of sin they came from.

The soul is the "gearbox" used by the spirit to do what the spirit wills to do in the physical world. The integration of soul and spirit is most evident when one begins to examine the mind/brain interface that allows the spirit of man to do physical activity in a physical world. As we all know, the brain is a physical part of the human body because if it is impaired or damaged, a brain surgeon can operate on it allowing him or her to do physical things to it. On the other hand, the mind is not physically accessible because it is spiritual and connected to our spirits.

While on earth, the stress between the spiritual attributes of mankind and the physical aspects of mankind is evident as we struggle to understand the inspirations flowing from emotions, feelings, attitudes, and thoughts.

The body is basically a neutral vehicle of expression used by the spirit and soul to interact with the physical world; therefore, the soul becomes the target for both God and the devil to take up residence in. Once the spirit is born-again, it is now regenerated allowing the Lord to make the human spirit His habitation. He then begins to purify and cleanse the soul in order to use it to express Himself. This process is called sanctification, which is the process of making something clean or holy. Remember, the Bible states in 1 Corinthians 6 that "the body is for the Lord and the Lord is for the body" making it clear to us that our bodies are not our own, they "have been bought with a price".

Spirit

The word translated "spirit" in the Bible is the Greek word *pneuma* which has the basic meaning of "air in motion" or "breath" necessary for life. The Spirit of God breathed His spirit into the nostrils of Adam, and he turned a clay man into a living and breathing human being.

And the Lord God formed man of the dust of the ground and breathed into his nostrils the breath of life; and man became a living being. (Genesis 2:7)

The Process

The impartation of God's spirit into Adam inspired this lifeless clay man to become a "living being" or as the King James Version of the Bible states, "a living soul."

As discussed earlier, man lives in a body, he has a soul, and he is a spirit. Although separate, these three integral parts operate in unison which sometimes makes it hard to determine the real purposes and intents of individuals we interact with as Christians. This is why we must examine each part separately to get a better understanding of the dynamics of man. When dealing with human beings, there is a tendency to forget that the human body only *houses* the human while not actually *being* the human. This is something that is extremely hard to get accustomed to because the five senses are always interacting with other people in the physical world, but the final reality is never found in the physical world. Man is a spirit, living in a body, using a soul to express himself through the body to the environment.

When Christians are born-again, God regenerates or reinspires the spirit of a person resurrecting the human spirit out from the dead. God breathes His Spirit back into us awakening us from a deep sleep caused by participation in sin. Satan has designed an earthly amusement park (which we refer to as "the matrix") designed to entertain and captivate the human soul preventing it from knowing it is enslaved within the confines of a prison planet. When we awaken from this state of suspended animation, the Holy Spirit begins the process of renovating the soul to make it able to accommodate God's presence. The Spirit of God goes to work transforming the mind, renewing our thinking, renovating our feelings and emotions, and getting rid of negative affectations like hatred, fear, guilt, shame, condemnation, lust, and perversion. The Bible calls this process restoration in Psalm 23:

A Psalm of David. The Lord is my shepherd; I shall not want. He makes me lie down in green pastures; He leads me beside the still waters. He restores my soul; He leads me in the paths of righteousness For His name's sake. (Psalm 23:1-3)

The Celestial Church consists of people who have gone through the restorative process enabling them to join

God's family of obedient children who no longer desire to rebel against their heavenly Father.

Therefore, brethren, we are debtors—not to the flesh, to live according to the flesh. For if you live according to the flesh you will die; but if by the Spirit you put to death the deeds of the body, you will live. For as many as are led by the Spirit of God, these are sons of God. For you did not receive the spirit of bondage again to fear, but you received the Spirit of adoption by whom we cry out, "Abba, Father." The Spirit Himself bears witness with our spirit that we are children of God, and if children, then heirs—heirs of God and joint heirs with Christ, if indeed we suffer with Him, that we may also be glorified together. (Romans 8:12-17)

The process of transformation is centrally focused on renovating the soul reformatting it to be interactive with a holy God while no longer being bound to Satan's matrix through the five carnal senses. It is necessary to have the soul reprogrammed to interface with God's Spirit allowing us to be integrated into the Body of Christ productively fulfilling the will of God in our lives. So many Christians have wasted so much time religiously adhering to the dictates of church organizations while negating the organic growth within themselves. Church and denominational memberships are designed to focus the mind on the outside, when in fact, the Kingdom of Heaven does not come with observation because it grows organically inside of individuals submitted to the process. The Holy Spirit is seeking out "Celestial People" who are sick and tired of playing religious games opting rather to be changed internally in order to plug into God's "Celestial Church". A transformed mind is the key that opens the door, finally liberating your soul from years of limitations and imprisonment imposed upon you by the warden that rules the matrix, Satan!

CHAPTER 10

The Celestial Church in Heaven

Now I saw a new heaven and a new earth, for the first heaven and the first earth had passed away. Also, there was no more sea. Then I, John, saw the holy city, New Jerusalem, coming down out of heaven from God, prepared as a bride adorned for her husband. And I heard a loud voice from heaven saying, "Behold, the tabernacle of God is with men, and He will dwell with them, and they shall be His people. God Himself will be with them and be their God. And God will wipe away every tear from their eyes; there shall be no more death, nor sorrow, nor crying. There shall be no more pain, for the former things have passed away." (Revelation 21:1-4)

Revelation 21 reveals the final climax achieved after submitting to the process – the Celestial Church is worshiping around the throne of God and all the death and sorrow experienced on the earth is gone forever. The born-again life of a believer culminates in eternity and at that time everything we have experienced in our lives will make perfect sense to us. God in His infinite wisdom has designed a plan to get us home, while simultaneously showing us why it is to our benefit to faithfully submit to His Kingdom's principles and authority. Heaven is the final destination for every believer that faithfully submits to the transformational process and individuals must remain steadfast and committed to following the steps necessary to arrive safely home.

The process of sanctification separates the Body of Christ from all the defiling elements designed by Satan to deter us away from our journey. Christians are commanded to "endure to the end" which means staying faithful throughout the many rigorous encounters we must experience in order to conform our souls to Jesus Christ. The process takes us through phases beginning with conception, followed by gestation, and finally ending with the manifestation of the finished product.

The metamorphosis of a Christian is a supernatural occurrence that can only be accomplished by the Holy Spirit, but it requires the daily cooperation of the born-again believer. Some believers have been made to believe that God changes us without our participation and any teaching that states Christians need to cooperate with the process is just theology based on "works". There are far too many if/then statements in the Bible for this misinterpretation of scripture to be true. A cursory reading of the Bible immediately reveals that most of the promises made to Christians are conditional requiring a response from the believer; therefore, any attempt to stamp participation as "works" is misguided and lacks understanding of the scriptures. The Bible reveals to us that we have been saved through the blood shed on the cross by Jesus Christ, we are being sanctified unto holiness by the washing of the word of God, and we will be eternally saved once we arrive in heaven. The sanctification process, which results in our transformation, requires that we cooperate with the Holy Spirit.

The purpose of transformation is to prepare us for our lives in heaven by starting the process while we are still on Earth. Where does this process begin? In the minds of believers that set their affections above and not on the earth according to Colossians 3:

Set your mind on things above, not on things on the earth. For you died, and your life is hidden with Christ in God. When Christ who is our life appears, then you also will appear with Him in glory. (Colossians 3:2-4)

The transformation of the mind spoken of in Romans 12:1-2 reveals the fact that God has made provisions for Christians to live on earth with minds that have been programmed to interact with His mind via the Holy Spirit. This is a great mystery, but Romans 8 discusses this in detail:

There is therefore now no condemnation to those who are in Christ Jesus, who do not walk according to the flesh, but according to the Spirit. For the law of the Spirit of life in Christ Jesus has made me free from the law of sin and death. For what the law could not do in that it was weak through the flesh, God did by sending His own Son in the likeness of sinful flesh, on account of sin: He condemned sin in the flesh, that the righteous requirement of the law might be fulfilled in us who do not walk according to the flesh but according to the

Spirit. For those who live according to the flesh set their minds on the things of the flesh, but those who live according to the Spirit, the things of the Spirit. For to be carnally minded is death, but to be spiritually minded is life and peace. Because the carnal mind is enmity against God; for it is not subject to the law of God, nor indeed can be. So then, those who are in the flesh cannot please God. But you are not in the flesh but in the Spirit, if indeed the Spirit of God dwells in you. Now if anyone does not have the Spirit of Christ, he is not His. And if Christ is in you, the body is dead because of sin, but the Spirit is life because of righteousness. But if the Spirit of Him who raised Jesus from the dead dwells in you, He who raised Christ from the dead will also give life to your mortal bodies through His Spirit who dwells in you. Therefore, brethren, we are debtors—not to the flesh, to live according to the flesh. For if you live according to the flesh you will die; but if by the Spirit you put to death the deeds of the body, you will live. For as many as are led by the Spirit of God, these are sons of God. For you did not receive the spirit of bondage again to fear, but you received the Spirit of adoption by whom we cry out, "Abba, Father." The Spirit Himself bears witness with our spirit that we are children of God, and if children, then heirs—heirs of God and joint heirs with Christ, if indeed we suffer with Him, that we may also be glorified together. (Romans 8:1-17)

As stated earlier, the journey is a three-step process. We are progressively moving from the flesh (Egypt), through our souls (the wilderness) and finally arriving in the spirit (the Promised Land). This entire journey is centrally focused on which arena the mind has been programmed to be consciously aware of. If the mind of a Christian focuses on the flesh, that individual will be world conscious. If the Christian focuses on the soul, then that individual will be self-conscious. But, if the Christian focuses on the spirit, he or she will be God-conscious. Always remember, the target is the soul and the elements contained therein; namely, the will, the emotions, the feelings, and the most important area of all, your thoughts.

When we start the salvation journey from flesh to spirit, we pick up an internal warfare. This internal warfare of the Christian has been given very little emphasis in most cases when ministers present the word of God, but it is imperative that the Body of Christ be made aware of the inner conflict initiated by salvation. Paul spoke of this conflict in Romans 7:

For we know that the law is spiritual, but I am carnal, sold under sin. For what I am doing, I do not understand. For what I will to do, that I do not practice; but what I hate, that I do. If then, I do what I will not to do, I agree with the law that it is good. But now, it is no longer I who do it, but sin that dwells in me. For I know that in me (that is, in my flesh) nothing good dwells; for to will is present with me, but how to perform what is good I do not find. For the good that I will to do, I do not do; but the evil I will not to do, that I practice. Now if I do what I will not to do, it is no longer I who do it, but sin that dwells in me. I find then a law, that evil is present with me, the one who wills to do good. For I delight in the law of God according to the inward man. But I see another law in my members, warring against the law of my mind, and bringing me into captivity to the law of sin which is in my members. O wretched man that I am! Who will deliver me from this body of death? I thank God—through Jesus Christ our Lord! (Romans 7:14-24)

The scripture also states in Galatians 5:

I say then: Walk in the Spirit, and you shall not fulfill the lust of the flesh. For the flesh lusts against the Spirit, and the Spirit against the flesh; and these are contrary to one another, so that you do not do the things that you wish. But if you are led by the Spirit, you are not under the law. Now the works of the flesh are evident, which are: adultery, fornication, uncleanness, lewdness, idolatry, sorcery, hatred, contentions, jealousies, outbursts of wrath, selfish ambitions, dissensions, heresies, envy, murders, drunkenness, revelries, and the like; of which I tell you beforehand, just as I also told you in time past, that those who practice such things will not inherit the kingdom of God. (Galatians 5:16-21)

The tension that exists between the flesh and the spirit is designed to keep us focused on the final objective, making heaven our eternal home. Through Jesus Christ,

The Process

God has imparted the power Christians need through the Holy Ghost enabling us to stand amid a wicked and perverse world without succumbing to the temptations found here. It doesn't take long for born-again believers to realize that after salvation a ferocious battle begins in the mind because Satan is trying to compel us to abandon the new life we just received from God. The power contained in the word of God equips us to make it through these satanically inspired battles by keeping our focus on heaven and not the earth. This takes tremendous discipline, and the four tools outlined in this book, the word of God, fasting, prayer and praise, and worship, are given to aid us as we fight our way back home to heaven. The Celestial Church in Heaven will be made up of those who endured to the end desiring a relationship with Jesus Christ above anything this world has to offer. I invite you to embrace the process by determining within the inner sanctums of your heart and soul, that you will endure until the end refusing to let anyone or anything deter you away from your final destination, HEAVEN!

Epilogue: Summary of the Process

In conclusion, I hope that this book has been a blessing to those who have read it and you have been inspired to "press on toward the prize" that God has promised to all believers. The four elements of the process will enhance your abilities to withstand Satan's attacks and the temptations and allure of this world. As with all organic life, whatever you feed the most will tend to grow stronger and expand its influence; therefore, it is necessary for Christians to feed the spirit at the expense of the soul and the flesh. Jesus said, "If anyone desires to come after Me, let him deny himself, and take up his cross, and follow Me. For whoever desires to save his life will lose it, but whoever loses his life for My sake will find it." (Matthew 16-24-25)

It is God's will that every Christian grows to maturity to carry the gospel to the ends of the earth. He has promised to be with us and to lead and guide us as we endeavor to do His will. *The Process* is a book written to help individual Christians achieve their maximum potential when they finally decide to embrace all that the Lord Jesus Christ has in store for them. It is my prayer that everyone who reads this book accepts the challenge to get out of the comfort zones of religion daring to "walk on the water" with the Lord accomplishing exploits that they never dreamed possible. I believe inside of every one of you there exists a "river of living water" that will release the anointing needed to turn millions to Jesus Christ. Just tell yourself that this time I will not be a spectator watching the game, but I choose to be a participator in the game. Just let the process take hold of you by setting your mind in heavenly places allowing the Lord to have access and He will do the rest. God bless you and keep you are my prayers.

Thank You

Thank you for reading The Process!

If you enjoyed this book, please consider writing a review with your honest impressions on Rempublish, Amazon, Goodreads, or another platform you choose. Your feedback is incredibly valuable for helping independent authors like us reach a wider audience.

RM
Remnant Media
PUBLICATIONS

CHECK OUT REMNANT MEDIA PUBLICATION'S OTHER BOOKS/RESOURCES!

WWW.REMPUBLISH.COM

GOD'S CELESTIAL NETWORK: *UNLOCK YOUR FULL POTENTIAL IN GOD'S KINGDOM WITH THE PRACTICAL 'SDOM CONTAINED IN THIS BOOK. DISCOVER THE KEY TO IVING A MAXIMIZED LIFE AND UNDERSTAND YOUR TRUE ODLY IDENTITY. ORDER NOW AND START YOUR JOURNEY TOWARDS A LIFE OF PURPOSE AND FULFILLMENT.*

WWW.REMPUBLISH.COM

ORGANIC GOSPEL: WHAT IF YOU REALIZED THAT THE GOSPEL JESUS CHRIST IS NOT CENTRALLY FOCUSED ON "DOING" THE WILL OF GOD, BUT "BECOMING" THE WILL OF GOD?

:AD THE ORGANIC GOSPEL AND FINALLY UNDERSTAND WHAT ALVATION IS REALLY ABOUT... MAYBE FOR THE FIRST TIME IN YOUR LIFE.

WWW.REMPUBLISH.COM

IE JESUS CULT: II CORINTHIANS 11:4 WARNS THAT SOME WILL USE THE NAME OF "JESUS" TO DRAW)PLE AWAY FROM JESUS CHRIST, THE SON OF GOD. HE JESUS CULT" EXAMINES THE FALSE DOCTRINES SED TO PROMOTE "ANOTHER GOSPEL" WHICH IS ESIGNED TO LEAD YOU TO THE WORSHIPPING OF IOTHER JESUS" BY USHERING IN "ANOTHER SPIRIT" TO THE CHURCH.

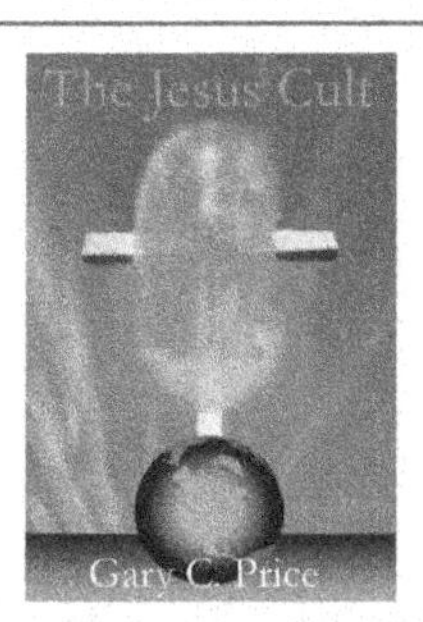

www.ingramcontent.com/pod-product-compliance
Lightning Source LLC
Chambersburg PA
CBHW052109090426
42741CB00009B/1738

* 9 7 9 8 9 8 9 2 9 3 7 9 7 *